BUSES
YEARBOOK 2020

Edited by STEWART J. BROWN

BUSES

YEARBOOK 2020

FRONT COVER: *First Glasgow has invested heavily in ADL products. This Enviro400 MMC was delivered in 2018.* SJB

THIS PAGE: *Looking like an arty London photo where the bus is rendered red against a monochrome background, this is a full-colour view of New Routemaster LT244 (LTZ 1244) in Cheapside where the surroundings just happen to be black and white.* JOHN ROBINSON

BACK COVER (UPPER): *Following the 2013 takeover by Stagecoach of First's Chester services the buses which changed hands received Stagecoach fleetnames on First's livery.* CLIFF BEETON

BACK COVER (LOWER): *Unusual types to be found until recently on London's outskirts included Metrobus MANs with MCV bodies.* SJB

PREVIOUS PAGE: *Go North East Optare Versa 8337 (NK11 HKP) with Quaylink branding at The Baltic Arts Centre in Gateshead.* RICHARD WALTER

Published by
Key Publishing Ltd
www.keypublishing.com

ISBN: 978 1 912205 95 0

Printed in Wales by **Gomer Press Ltd**
Llandysul Enterprise Park
Llandysul, Ceredigion SA44 4JL

www.busesmag.com

A left-hand-drive Alexander Dennis Enviro500 SuperLo, built to fit beneath North American overbridges and street furniture. It is 3.91m (12ft 10in) high and carries up to 81 passengers.

All photographs by the author.

Guildford grasscutter to global giant

Buses magazine editor ALAN MILLAR charts the 15-year story of Alexander Dennis, the UK's largest bus and coach builder.

As I write this in June 2019, news has broken of the sale of Alexander Dennis — the UK's biggest bus manufacturer — to the Canadian-based NFI Group for £320million, marking another milestone in the story of a business that has grown spectacularly at home and abroad since it was created in conditions of adversity in 2004.

Its achievements are especially impressive when compared with where its three main component parts — Dennis, Alexander and Plaxton — were half a century ago.

By the end of the 1960s, it seemed unbelievable that Dennis would ever build another bus. Dennis Bros had been around since 1897, based then as now in Guildford, renowned once for its output of lawnmowers, still for fire engines and dustcarts.

It had been a significant bus manufacturer before World War Two, supplying municipal and company

BELOW: *A preserved example of one of the first post-war combinations of Alexander body and Dennis chassis. This 1962 Loline III for Dennis's local BET group operator, Aldershot & District, has the Scottish coachbuilder's G-type body.* ALL PHOTOGRAPHS BY THE AUTHOR.

A TransBus Enviro300 with Cardiff Bus.

operators, but lost its way when peacetime returned. It might have quit building buses much sooner had it not struck a deal with state-owned Bristol to build its revolutionary low height double-deck Lodekka under licence from 1956, calling its version the Loline and selling it into the wider market that Bristol was prevented from supplying.

It enjoyed modest success, but as operators embraced rear-engined designs, Dennis had nothing to offer. The last of 281 Lolines were delivered early in 1967. One final blast — more like a spurt — came the following year when the local authority in Llandudno bought two single-deckers based on Pax V truck chassis for a route that scaled the Great Orme.

With most other British manufacturers of heavy-duty buses by then absorbed into the newly created British Leyland, it looked like Dennis's day had passed. It would go on building fire engines and dustcarts but had its bus route terminated with two Pax Vs on a Welsh headland?

Life, however, was on the up for bodybuilders Alexander and Plaxton. Alexander had been building buses since 1924 and met a large part of the state-owned Scottish Bus Group's requirements.

It broadened its customer base from the 1950s, particularly into the municipal sector and British Electric Traction (BET) fleets in England and opened a large new factory in Falkirk in 1958. It acquired the Belfast coachbuilder, Potters, in 1969 and became the principal bodybuilder for the state-owned Ulsterbus fleet.

Its BET customers included Aldershot & District and North Western, which bought G-type bodies on Dennis Loline chassis in the early 1960s, the first post-war examples of an Alexander Dennis combination.

Threats nevertheless lay on the horizon. The state-owned National Bus Company took over the BET companies, had a 50% shareholding in British Leyland's three bodybuilding subsidiaries and in the Leyland National joint venture to mass-produce complete vehicles, starting with a single-decker. That had the potential to starve independent bodybuilders like Alexander of a supply of chassis. Alexander's orders from NBC soon diminished to a fraction of what it had enjoyed with BET.

Plaxton, based in Scarborough from foundation in 1907, started making coach bodies after World War One. By the end of the 1960s, it had overtaken

Duple to become the country's largest coach body builder. It also built buses, typically in small quantities and in the summer months when a reduced workforce was kept on after building the season's new coaches. The 'surplus' labour typically took summer jobs catering for the thousands of visitors to the Yorkshire resort.

The end of TransBus

The landscape had changed by 31 March, 2004 when TransBus International, a four-year-old business incorporating Dennis, Alexander and Plaxton, went into administration.

TransBus was owned 70% by Mayflower, a financially overstretched automotive engineering group that had acquired Alexander in 1995 and Dennis in 1998, and 30% by Henlys, the former car retailing group that had been merged with Plaxton

in 1989.

Dennis had returned to buses in the mid-1970s, building niche products like the Dominator double-decker to plug gaps created when Leyland rationalised its range, then struck gold in 1989 with the Dart, a simply engineered lightweight single-decker with Cummins engine and Allison gearbox that addressed the strengths and weaknesses of the van- and light truck-derived minibuses then in vogue. Its low-floor Trident double-decker, also with Cummins engine, followed in 1998.

Plaxton had become a year-round builder of buses, particularly with the Pointer body that was the most popular built on the Dart, and in 1995 had acquired Wigan-based Northern Counties to take it into the double-deck market. TransBus scaled Plaxton down to an all-year coach manufacturer in 2001, transferring Pointer production to the Alexander plant at Falkirk.

Alexander, Dennis, Northern Counties and Plaxton had all benefited from the demise of British Leyland. Volvo had acquired what was left of Leyland Bus in 1988 and within four years had closed most of that, including its remaining bodybuilding capacity. Dennis and Alexander had both developed export business in Hong Kong and Singapore, and TransBus had begun to break into North America with some small, but significant wins.

As news of the TransBus collapse sunk in, rumours circulated that the administrators were in discussions with Chinese manufacturers, private equity firms and others who might not be too troubled about keeping bus design and manufacturing expertise in the British Isles.

The good news in May 2004 was not just that the business was sold to UK buyers, but that the two sets of new owners were already familiar with what they were buying, cared deeply about their purchases and were committed to keeping them in Britain.

A management buyout led by former TransBus executive Brian Davidson, backed by venture capitalists, paid £10.5million for the Plaxton coach business centred on the Scarborough factory and the dealership, repair facility and small vehicle manufacturing operation at Anston, south of Sheffield.

LEFT: *One of the TransBus Enviro200 prototypes from 2003, photographed nearly 10 years later with Buses Excetera. The offside rear engine allowed it to have a 100% low floor and a rear rather than centre door.*

TransBus had gradually extinguished the Alexander, Dennis and Plaxton brand names, though the coach factory had defied that edict to continue fixing embossed Plaxton rear number plate frames on the backs of its products. The new owners proudly revived the name and adopted a logo based on the outline of Scarborough Castle.

Days later, a Scottish consortium concluded the £90million acquisition of most of what was left of TransBus to create Alexander Dennis. Its shareholders were Stagecoach founders Brian Souter and Ann Gloag, financier Sir Angus Grossart and businessman Sir David Murray, whose Murray International Metals was a major supplier (he later sold his interest to the other shareholders). Stagecoach had been a loyal customer, particularly of Alexander bodywork, since the late 1980s.

It bought the Guildford, Falkirk and Wigan factories, a parts centre in Skelmersdale and five service centres, but not the Belfast plant, which closed. Two former Alexander managing directors from Mayflower days, Bill Cameron and Jim Hastie, returned as chairman and chief executive respectively.

Two ranges

At the time, Plaxton built three full-size coaches mainly on Volvo chassis: the Panther, Paragon and Profile; and two small vehicles on the Mercedes-Benz Vario light truck chassis: the Beaver 2 midibus and Cheetah midicoach. All have stainless steel structures. Over the three years after the buyout, it developed a wheelchair accessible version of the Profile, a 15m high-capacity Panther and a stylish second-generation Cheetah.

It also returned to the single-deck bus market, reopening the mothballed Pointer production hall in Scarborough to build the Centro on VDL, Volvo and MAN chassis and fit out the integral rear-engined Primo midibus — intended as a low-floor replacement for the Beaver 2 — using powered shells built in Hungary by Enterprise Bus, another remnant of TransBus.

Alexander Dennis began life faced with an urgent need to stem continuing financial losses. Jobs still had to be shed, and some support facilities closed or relocated. It also concluded that there was insufficient work for the Wigan plant, which closed in January 2005 on completion of outstanding orders

A Plaxton Centro-bodied VDL SB120 of Arriva North West in Northwich in 2007. The SB120 was a Dart-influenced chassis developed primarily for Arriva.

for the President double-deck body built there.

TransBus had started developing a new bus range, with the Enviro300 large single-decker in 2001, Enviro500 tri-axle export double-decker in 2002 and had shown prototypes of a sophisticated successor to the Dart, the Enviro200, in 2003. Alexander Dennis inherited these along with the Pointer Dart, the Trident and two Alexander bodies from the late 1990s, the 12m ALX300 single-decker built mainly on MAN chassis for Stagecoach and the ALX400 double-decker built on the Trident and Volvo B7TL.

The ALX400 was starting to look its age and to many seemed bland by comparison with the Gemini that had taken Northern Ireland-based Wrightbus into the double-deck market for the first time in 2001.

An early priority, therefore, was to accelerate development of an Enviro400 home market double-decker ahead of the Enviro200. It was revealed in summer 2005, a distinctively styled creation with a chassis developed from the Trident and designed to accommodate as many lower saloon seats as possible. A reshaped fuel tank squeezed one of those seats between the staircase and driver's cab.

The Enviro400 body also was offered on Volvo chassis, though only 110 were built, 100 of them for Dublin Bus. Thanks mainly to orders from Stagecoach and Nottingham City Transport, it was built in significantly greater numbers on Scania N230UD chassis. In 2005, Dublin Bus bought 70 Enviro500 bodies on tri-axle Volvo B9TL chassis.

A simplified Enviro200 followed the next year, phased into production to replace the faithful Pointer Dart. Body styling was similar to the 2003 TransBus prototypes, but with the low-entry layout and T-drive of the Dart in place of the 2003 prototypes' full low-floor layout with front and rear doors. For a time, Alexander Dennis maintained customer familiarity by calling it the Enviro200 Dart.

Plaxton's independence ended shortly after the company's centenary celebration in April 2007. Its backers were looking for an exit and Alexander Dennis bought the business for an undisclosed sum. Most of TransBus was back together, but this deal kept the Plaxton name and provided Alexander Dennis with production capacity that it needed for future growth.

Brian Davidson joined Alexander Dennis in senior roles before leaving to pursue his entrepreneurial instincts in ventures that today include the group behind the Mellor minibus business in Rochdale.

Late examples of the TransBus President built at Wigan included this Volvo B7TL for Metroline.

An Alexander Dennis-built Pointer Dart in the Stagecoach East Midlands fleet.

Change at the top

The Plaxton purchase coincided with a change at the top of Alexander Dennis. Jim Hastie retired, succeeded as chief executive officer by Colin Robertson, now Colin Robertson CBE. Colin, a straight-talking son of Lanarkshire who had held senior positions with Terex, an American manufacturer of construction industry plant, had returned across the Atlantic and bought a significant minority shareholding in Alexander Dennis. He pledged to double the size of the business within five years. Bill Cameron remained chairman until his sudden death, aged 70, in October 2008.

Robertson's drive and energy has taken Alexander Dennis on an impressive growth path, with turnover up from £195million (solely in the UK and Far East) in 2004 to £631million in 2018, of which

The increasingly comprehensive Plaxton coach range includes the Elite-i inter-deck on tri-axle Volvo B11R chassis. This one is operated by Acklams of Beverley.

An Enviro400 for Stagecoach London nearing completion at the Falkirk factory in 2013.

£281million came from overseas sales. It earned profits of £24.4million in 2017 and £28.2million in 2018. If it realises its international ambitions, it will be generating over £1billion turnover by 2022.

Under his leadership, it has broadened its product range, embraced recent technology, won new home market customers and export orders across four continents.

The Centro and Primo were dropped within three years, but investment at Scarborough has turned much of its production capacity over to Alexander Dennis buses — Enviro200s in the single-deck assembly hall and Enviro400s on two of the four production lines in what had been the coach plant; Scarborough has also assembled Enviro400 chassis.

The Enviro300 was updated in 2007, with chassis modifications as well as body changes to reflect the family look of the Enviro200. The Enviro300 body also was adapted for third party chassis, mainly for Stagecoach, initially to replace the ALX300 on the MAN 18.240, later on the Scania K230UB when MAN fell out of favour with the UK's largest operator. There also were 45 on Volvo B7RLEs for Ulsterbus, and in 2008/09 it built 95 Enviro200 bodies on the MAN 14.240 chassis, 82 of them for Stagecoach.

The quest for new driveline technology picked up where TransBus left off with the prototype Enviro200s, reactivating a partnership with Sheffield-based Magnetic Systems Technology — better known as Magtec — to produce hybrid single- and double-deckers. It came up with a brand name — Ecoturas, combining the first three letters of ecology with a Scots Gaelic word for journey — when announcing this in November 2006.

One year on, it had dropped Magtec in favour of BAE Systems, whose United States-built HybriDrive system was already installed in 2,000 North American transit buses, matched to the four-cylinder version of the Cummins ISB engine. The first Enviro200H hybrids appeared in 2009, the Enviro400H double-deck equivalent following in 2010 and proving particularly popular in London.

The same driveline went into the 12m Enviro350H, a full low-floor single-decker produced in 2010-13 and developed for the Spanish market with left-hand-drive, in-line engine in the rear left-hand corner and provision for three doors. Twelve with Tata Hispano bodywork went to Barcelona, while Stagecoach and First bought 26 right-hand-drive one-door versions with Alexander Dennis bodywork.

There might also have been a double-deck equivalent, maybe an Enviro450H, with engine in the right-hand-corner had Alexander Dennis succeeded in its bid to build Transport for London's three-door twin staircase New Routemaster in 2009, a competition in which it was disappointed to lose out to Wrightbus, not least because the purchase of an eventual fleet of 1,000 New Routemasters would depress the London operators' ability to order other double-deckers.

Major Model Change

By 2014, with Euro6 emission standards demanding major driveline investment, Robertson was leading a project called Major Model Change — MMC for short — to replace the product line-up. MMC was an internal code name, but key customers were consulted throughout the product development process and took to using the three letters to distinguish the new models from the ones they replaced.

The new Enviro400 (and its Enviro500 export equivalent), while recognisably influenced by the style of the 2005 model, is a different beast. Wrap-round windscreens radically alter the appearance of the new Enviro200, which also replaced the Enviro300.

In 2015, it answered Transport for London's call for New Routemaster styling on other double-deckers by developing the Enviro400 City with glazed staircase, rounded front with shallower upper deck windscreen, available initially only on the Enviro400H. Far more have been sold outside London on non-hybrid chassis.

Since then, the hybrid offering has been broadened, with potentially longer life super-capacitors in place of batteries on the Enviro400H and a 48v SmartHybrid version that achieves fuel and emissions savings with less complexity and cost. There also is an Enviro400FC, with zero-emission hydrogen fuel-cell technology, and an extended range hybrid that runs mainly in electric mode.

For the UK and some export markets (New Zealand and probably Hong Kong), Alexander Dennis has formed a joint venture with Chinese battery and electric vehicle manufacturer BYD to build electric Enviro200s and Enviro400s on BYD chassis. The Enviro400EV has the City body.

It met UK demand for biogas buses by cooperating with Scania, initially with the K270UB chassis and Enviro300 body, later with the N280UD double-decker with the Enviro400, most of which have the City body.

Blackpool Transport has taken several batches of the Enviro400 City as part of a fleet modernisation programme based entirely on Alexander Dennis products.

A BYD/Alexander Dennis Enviro200EV battery electric demonstrator displayed at the Euro Bus Expo show in November 2018.

The Enviro400 has also been adapted for two Volvo chassis: the B5LH hybrid, of which 83 have gone to Go-Ahead London and Stagecoach; and as the Enviro400XLB on the tri-axle B8L diesel introduced towards the end of 2018 and sold so far to Lothian and Stagecoach, Lothian being a customer won back from Wrightbus to which it turned after the TransBus collapse.

Other customers won from competing manufacturers include Trent Barton, Transdev Blazefield, Go North East, Go South Coast and Brighton & Hove. First Bus has also become a major customer and in 2009 took the only 25 Enviro500s built for the UK.

Plaxton adds choice

Plaxton has continued to broaden its range. While the Paragon was discontinued, the Panther has been given two facelifts and made available in more lengths including a short wheelbase Panther Cub on Volvo B8R chassis.

The top-of-the-range Elite was added in 2008, originally as a touring coach, later also in a scheduled express service format. The Leopard, a 2.5m wide body developed originally for Australia where it would have been sold on an MAN chassis, replaced the Profile as the entry level coach in the range in 2013. The inter-deck Elite *i* arrived in 2012, followed in 2018 by the low-entry Panther LE (based on the Leopard but with Panther front styling) and Panorama double-decker.

It also scaled down the Leopard to create the Cheetah XL body launched in 2015 to fill the gap left by Mercedes-Benz's decision to stop building the Vario van. This was based on the larger Atego truck.

Products were not the only assets to come with the purchase of Plaxton. Its sales team was well experienced in meeting the needs of smaller operators, for coaches and buses, and Alexander Dennis has harnessed this expertise to take a growing share of the retail market for buses — often single vehicles or batches of ones and twos — to smaller operators that previously went elsewhere.

This is a huge cultural change from 40 and 50 years ago, when independent operators' Alexander orders were invariably tagged on to bigger batches for major customers with no opportunity for these small customers to choose even the colour of fabric on the seats.

Tri-axle drives exports

The product that has transformed Alexander Dennis's place in the world is the tri-axle Enviro500, with which it has sold the concept of high capacity double-deckers in markets where they were largely unknown.

The process began before Alexander Dennis came into existence, but its determination and patience have paid off, building on the groundwork of producing this vehicle for the demanding conditions of Hong Kong, then a series of variants for the United States and Canada, where height restrictions require lower vehicles for commuter services.

It won a 90-vehicle order from Mexico City — against global competition — for a bus rapid transit service, has sold Enviro500s in Singapore, Malaysia, New Zealand, Switzerland (to two customers) and in 2018 won a contract to build at least 200, and possibly as many as 430, for Berlin.

Although all are called Enviro500s, there are big differences in the vehicles built for these different markets, not just in interior layout and overall height, but also in their drivelines. Not all engines are in the same position, nor necessarily are all of them powered by Cummins. The first electric versions — with Allison driveline and Proterra batteries rather than a BYD chassis — go to a United States customer in 2020.

Alexander Dennis factories build these British-designed products in the United States, Canada, China and Malaysia, and local assembly is also planned to deliver the Berlin order. Kiwi Bus Builders has assembled Enviro200s for New Zealand, where Plaxton has supplied the Elite body on tri-axle Scania chassis.

The United States plant in Nappanee, Indiana also builds the Enviro200, which NFI built from 2012 to 2017 as the New Flyer MiDi in a joint venture that first brought the two companies together.

It tried breaking into the Australian market in 2012 when it acquired the Custom Coach bodybuilding business, but incurred losses and pulled out in 2014. Future export ambitions are focused on the Americas, Europe, Asia, Australasia and parts of the Middle East, and NFI Group — which had no presence outside North America — has placed its faith in Colin Robertson and Alexander Dennis to continue taking products like the Enviro500 across the globe.

The takeover gives the Alexander Dennis shareholders — Sir Brian Souter, Dame Ann Gloag, Sir Angus Grossart, Colin Robertson and chief financial officer Michael Stewart — a stake in the enlarged NFI Group, as they have invested 10% of their proceeds from the sale in shares in the Canadian company.

One of the Enviro500 success stories has been to sell 19 three-door, twin-staircase models to PostAuto in Switzerland. The third of the order was exhibited at Busworld in Kortrijk, Belgium in October 2017.

All photographs by the author.

A Colourful Revival

Richard Walter celebrates the growing variety of bus liveries, from route branding to heritage colour schemes.

As someone who grew up in the 1960s and 1970s, I have fond memories of the wealth of colourful liveries up and down the length of the UK. Every city and town had its own identity stamped on its buses and coaches and route branding started to be introduced to help encourage passengers along some of the busiest and most profitable routes.

The deregulation of bus services in the 1980s saw some sweeping changes as gradually most companies were consumed by the big bus groups - Stagecoach, First, Arriva, National Express and Go-Ahead. The resultant corporate liveries replaced the traditional colours in many places and Britain's bus scene became much less interesting to enthusiasts and, indeed, the travelling public. Only a handful of municipal operators held out, keeping their traditional looks.

Route branding changed over the next twenty years or so. Initially the big groups did not wish their liveries to be spoiled by too complicated or intrusive designs and incorporated wording applied to their existing colours. The increasing use of vinyl wraps however made it easier to remove or amend branding as routes changed or buses were transferred to other parts of the group.

Over the last few years, that has all changed. Stagecoach retains a version of its blue white and red colours but makes use of sides, and particularly the rears of vehicles through mega rear vinyl displays, to identify route and fare information alongside other features such as on-board Wi-Fi and season tickets.

First has changed its livery several times and now favours using distinct colours swooping over the fronts of vehicles and giant route numbers to

LEFT: *Lothian Buses decided to forego route branding which had been featured on many key city services over the years and instead adopted a corporate style livery in different colour variations for its various operations throughout the Lothians. ADL Enviro400XLB-bodied Volvo B8L 1080 (SJ19 OWV), one of the first batch of 100-seat tri-axle buses to enter service in March 2019, is wearing the Edinburgh City variation of madder and white. It was pictured on Frogston Road, Edinburgh, on service 11. These 13.4m-long buses have 350bhp Volvo D8K engines.*

BELOW: *Route branding took off in Reading in a big way from 2004 with specific colours being adopted for most routes. At the end of 2017 Reading Buses took over Green Line route 702 from First. Before settling on its own distinctive green livery, buses from the multi-coloured fleet operated the service. ADL Enviro400 MMC 759 (YY15 OYA) is one of a number in a generic grey livery. It is approaching Victoria in London in October 2018.*

ABOVE: *Route branding was largely discontinued in Central London some years ago with vehicles from the various operators appearing in all over red. Wearing vinyls explaining its unique features and brightening up its appearance, Go-Ahead London has been trialling TA1 (LX18 DGF), a 78-seat BCI Enterprise Vantage hybrid on route 12 from Camberwell Garage. It is seen reaching its terminal point at Oxford Circus in January 2019.*

BELOW: *Xplore Dundee Volvo B7TL/Wrightbus Eclipse Gemini 7001 (SP54 CHF) pictured in the centre of Dundee in December 2018 sports a smart retro Dundee Corporation livery which suits the modern bus very well. The company is part of National Express.*

promote certain routes. Again, rear vinyl can be used to promote other information about either the company or the routes served.

National Express introduced Platinum and Emerald services using the same basic livery style but in assorted colours such as grey or red in Birmingham and green in Dundee. This replaced a bland white and red livery across all its bus companies. The front screens are highlighted by individual colours too, with the sides of buses showing stops along the routes and promoting legroom, Wi-Fi and other features.

Arriva introduced Sapphire services with leather seats and luxury fittings with essentially a two-tone blue livery on its single- and double-deck fleets.

Elsewhere in the places that the big groups are not the main operators, livery styles vary. All the operators in the central London area are obliged to keep to a traditional all-red livery. In Edinburgh

Lothian Buses has modernised its famous madder and white using a stylised version that has been adapted in blue and white, green and grey, and green and cream for its associated companies, Airlink, Skylink, East Coast Buses and Lothian Country. Reading Buses and Nottingham Buses use different liveries for all main routes. And in the north-east of England a variety of liveries and identities are worn by the buses of the Go-Ahead group.

As bus companies try to compete to win back passengers, it is unlikely that things will stand still, so changes in liveries will surely continue. An interesting development has been the repainting of vehicles in retro liveries in different parts of the country. Modern bodywork suits many of them well.

Now, what if this were a sign that some of the much-missed colours might make a full comeback in the future... ?

LEFT: *Optare Metrodecker 899 (YJ16 DFG) photographed arriving in London in July 2018 started service as a demonstrator in all-over blue but is now part of the Reading Buses fleet and was given this distinctive new-style Green Line livery with Windsor attractions branding. This is an 11.4m-long model powered by a four-cylinder Mercedes-Benz engine.*

BELOW: *Stagecoach uses its famous red, white and blue livery to promote local company services by adding side and rear vinyls. 54508 (YX18 LHU), a Volvo B8RLE with 53-seat Plaxton Panther LE body, is seen shortly after delivery in May 2018 on route X55, Dunfermline to Edinburgh.*

ABOVE: *Looking bright and colourful in November 2018 is First York Wrightbus-bodied Volvo B7RLE 69374 (YJ08 XYO) in Rider York heritage livery.*

LEFT: *National Express West Midlands has an assortment of colours on its fleet – several which are marketed as Platinum routes. The X1 and X2 were the first routes to be so branded on the Birmingham to Coventry corridor. ADL Enviro400 MMC 6845 (SN66 WFP) was pictured at Birmingham airport in October 2018.*

BELOW: *A good example of a traditional smart livery suiting a modern vehicle is Stagecoach Fife FD27532 (SV57 BYM), a 2007 ADL Enviro300 in Princes Street, Edinburgh, in September 2018. The livery marks 100 years of Dunfermline bus depot.*

ABOVE: *First has introduced an updated version of its livery throughout its UK operations. Some buses feature a generic version whilst others have brightly-coloured front swoops for vehicles allocated to particular routes. ADL Enviro400 MMC 33435 (SN66 WGF) shows off the First West Lothian colour for route 23/X23 between Edinburgh and Livingston/Broxburn in January 2019.*

RIGHT: *Go-North East Wrightbus Eclipse Gemini-bodied Volvo B7TL 3965 (574 CPT, previously NK06 JXB) sports the distinctive Angel livery on service 21 between Durham, Chester-Le-Street, Low Fell and Newcastle. Since the photo was taken in August 2017, new Wrightbus StreetDeck Micro Hybrids have replaced the Geminis.*

ABOVE: *East Yorkshire 814 (BF67 GHZ) is a Volvo B5TL with Egyptian-built MCV eVoSeti body. It uses the company's base livery with vinyl branding for service X46, Hull to York, although it appeared to be on service 45, Pocklington to York, when pictured in November 2018.*

ABOVE: *Displaying the latest version of the group's Sapphire livery is Arriva North East ADL Enviro400 MMC 7549 (YX17 NNZ) pulling into Haymarket Bus Station in Newcastle in August 2017.*

ABOVE: *First Glasgow ADL Enviro400 MMC 33207 (SK68 LWV) carries a yellow front for cross-city route 75, Milton to Castlemilk. It is turning from Union Street into Argyle Street in October 2018.*

BELOW: *Open-top tours have become popular throughout the UK. RATP's The Original Tour in London recently changed its livery to the colours of the Union Jack. This UNVI Urbis, PO68 CAX, is an electric bus and is in a green and white version of the Union Jack livery to stress its environmentally-friendly credentials. It is passing the Queen's Gallery in January 2019.*

The Great London Variety Show

The days of standard buses in London are long gone. **Gavin Booth** takes a look.

In 1953 the Booth family caught the 'Starlight Special' (Edinburgh Waverley to London Marylebone, overnight) for a holiday in London. This was a sightseeing trip at a time when I was still an active loco spotter, but by the time we returned to London in 1958 I knew a bit about London's buses from the blessed *Buses Illustrated* and the few books available to enthusiasts then, which were usually about London anyway.

I knew from my newly-acquired Ian Allan *ABC London Transport Buses, Coaches & Trolleybuses* that there were pages and pages devoted to the RT type – some 19 pages to list the 4,460 RTs that were in stock at the time – plus another nine pages listing the Leyland members of the family – the 1,560 RTLs and the 500 wider RTWs. And in Central London you couldn't help but be impressed by the high degree of standardisation that London Transport

The fount of all knowledge 60 years ago – the 1958 Ian Allan ABC London Transport Buses, Coaches & Trolleybuses, *price 2/6 (12½p), featuring on the cover RML3, the Leyland-engined, Weymann-bodied prototype that entered service in January 1958.*

All photographs by the author.

had achieved. My *ABC* told me these buses had a mix of Metro-Cammell, Park Royal, Saunders and Weymann bodies, and while the *cognoscenti* could probably distinguish one bodybuilder's product from the others, they all looked the same to me. I was only young, after all.

The *ABC* promised me other delights – 76 lowbridge AEC Regent III RLHs, dwindling batches of older T (AEC) and TD (Leyland) single-deckers, the 700 underfloor-engined AEC Regal IV RFs, the 84 little Guy GSs and the 65 BEA Regal IV coaches. Only the Green Line RFs and the BEA coaches seemed to penetrate the parts of London we explored and although I dragged my parents and sister to Surrey Docks terminus to seek – and find – RM1, the very first Routemaster, it would be some years before I was allowed to venture *sans* parents and sister to exotic places like Edgware (TD Tigers), Hemel Hempstead (GS Guys) or Northwick Park (lowbridge RLHs) to seek out a bit of variety.

Fast forward to the 2010s and the buses serving London are quite different, and remarkably varied. Transport for London (TfL) now defines the bus routes and specifies timetables, frequencies and fares. Commercial operators bid for routes when these come up for tender and often – but by no means always – retain them. The loss of a route has repercussions for staff, vehicles and even garages. TfL indicates what capacity is required and operators can include brand-new buses or existing buses in their bids. This is where the variety can come in as operators have their own favoured suppliers and will aim for standardisation, but on occasion will shop elsewhere to guarantee delivery of suitable buses in time for the start of a new contract.

Back in the 1950s there was never any doubt that every London bus would be built in the United Kingdom. With a range of UK chassis and body builders on hand, why would you go elsewhere? But in the 1970s and 1980s major manufacturers from mainland Europe gained a foothold in the UK while at the same time most of the major players over here were merging awkwardly under the Leyland banner.

Today's London operators can still buy on the home

LEFT: **Traditional Routemasters can be seen operating a heritage service which has been restricted to short workings of Stagecoach's 15 route between Trafalgar Square and the Tower of London in recent years and is being further cut back to run only on weekends and Bank Holidays. This 1964 bus is in the Strand in April 2017.**

The Plaxton President body was once a common sight in and around London, like this Go-Ahead 2002 10m example on Volvo B7TL chassis, seen in Croydon in April 2016. The President is now on the verge of extinction.

In the early days of the New Routemaster, in July 2013, two Metroline examples lay over at the Hampstead Heath terminus of route 24. LT11 on the left still carries its original registration mark, LK13 FJJ, before coming in line with its neighbour LT39 (LTZ 1039), with registration LTZ 1011.

Arriva has a large fleet of Wright Gemini 2DL 10.4m double-deckers, like this 2013 example on Waterloo Bridge in April 2017.

The Wrightbus Gemini 3 body is easily distinguished from the original version by its shallower upper deck windows. This 2015 Metroline 10.5m example on Volvo B5LH chassis is in Oxford Street in December 2016.

RIGHT: **Unique in the London fleet are Go-Ahead's 10.3m Optare Olympus-bodied ADL Tridents, new in 2008. This one at Kingston's Cromwell Road bus station in June 2017 is followed by an RATP London United ADL Enviro200 and a Go-Ahead Volvo B9TL/Wrightbus Gemini 2 in the livery of the East London Transit operation; as this is south-west London it is actually operating TfL's only all-day express service, the X26 between Heathrow Central and West Croydon.**

market, notably from Alexander Dennis, Optare and Wrightbus, but a quick flick through the London Omnibus Traction Society's invaluable *London Bus and Tram Fleetbook* – today's successor to those Ian Allan *ABCs* of yore – is a reminder that they are not only buying buses built in Europe but also bodies built in Egypt and even chassis built in China.

Interestingly, the number of buses in 2019 is not greatly changed from the 1958 figure – roundly 9,000. But in 1958 there were green London buses as well as the red London buses, where the green ones ventured way beyond today's Greater London area into the Home Counties. So there are many more red buses serving what is now defined as London, a consequence of high-frequency routes and the growing problems caused by traffic congestion. Increasing congestion and lower bus speeds often mean that more buses are required to maintain a high level of service.

So where do you find this 21st century variety?

Later Volvo B5LHs with Wrightbus Gemini 3 bodies have this squarer 'stealth' frontal treatment, as on a 10.6m London Sovereign 2016 example in the Strand in February 2017.

LEFT: *A 2008 10.2m ADL Enviro200 of Metroline leaves the busy Golders Green bus station in April 2016.*

BELOW: *A 2016 10.9m Abellio ADL Enviro200 MMC at Elephant & Castle in May 2016.*

Even in Central London there is plenty of choice – mostly double-deck but a good range of ADL, Volvo and Wrightbus types. ADL Enviro400s of course, in all their guises – diesel, hybrid, what can be termed Classic as well as the face-lifted MMC (Major Model Change) and E400 City styles. And loads of Volvo B9TL (diesel) and B5LH (hybrid) with Gemini bodies by Wrightbus, as well as an increasing number with Egyptian-built MCV eVoSeti bodies and even some with ADL bodies.

And there are full electric and hydrogen exotica to be found. The most popular electric type is the single-deck Chinese-built BYD (Build Your Dreams) D9UR with ADL Enviro200EV bodies in 10.8m and 12m form in the Go-Ahead and Metroline fleets. There are two Irizar electric buses in the Go-Ahead fleet as well as a Wrightbus StreetAir electric. Arguably more exotic, and certainly much rarer, are Tower Transit's hydrogen fuel cell buses – two Van Hools and eight VDL/Wrights. Electric double-deckers are still thin on the ground, but more are

on order to join Metroline's five BYD K10s - 37 ADL E400EV on BYD chassis during 2019.

ADL, Volvo and Wrightbus account for most of London's double-deckers and chassis makers and bodybuilders have had to keep reinventing their products to keep up with European emissions standards and to keep providing bodies that look attractive and up-to-date. The emissions standards have become increasingly stringent – from Euro I in 1992 through to the current London fleet which is now dominated by Euro V and Euro VI models with a growing interest in pure electric buses.

ADL concentrates on supplying complete double-deckers, although as we have seen there are ADL-bodied Volvos. The first ADL low-floor double-deck model was the ALX400 Trident, in London fleets from 1998 and now all but gone. This was replaced by the Enviro400 in 2005 and this has spawned the hybrid E400H, the virtual electric E400VE, the current E400 MMC (Major Model Change) and the E400 City.

Volvo's low-floor chassis were the B7TL, in London fleets from 1999, but its Euro V successor, the B9TL, can be found in many fleets along with a substantial number of the current hybrid B5LH.

Wrightbus burst on to the double-deck scene in 2001 with its arch-roofed Gemini body, which morphed into the 'smiley' Gemini 2 in 2008 and the Gemini 3 in 2014 with a more conventional front end

A rare 12m Optare Tempo of RATP London United at Hounslow in June 2016. It was new in 2011.

A 2012 Abellio ADL 10.1m Enviro400H at Clapham Junction in May 2016. It is a 61-seater.

Arriva operates nine Optare MetroCity electric buses on the 312 route linking South Croydon and Norwood Junction. New in 2014, one is seen picking up passengers in Croydon in April 2016.

A 2015 Arriva 10.4m ADL Enviro400 City approaches Tower Bridge in May 2018. This Londonized hybrid version of ADL's E400 has proved popular in other parts of the UK.

and then with the squarer 'stealth' front. These were built on VDL and Volvo chassis, but Wrightbus also produces complete double-deckers – the Gemini 2DL, built for Arriva around VDL components and most famously the New Routemaster – and there are also a small number of its integral StreetDeck model in London service.

I manage to visit London regularly enough to keep up with what's happening in Central London and it was interesting to note that on a recent bus trip from Waterloo to King's Cross every bus I encountered was a hybrid diesel-electric, a full electric or even a hydrogen bus. Not a pure diesel bus in sight.

But that's not always the case beyond the centre and I usually try to make time to venture on expeditions to the far-flung and not so far-flung suburbs, knowing that there are often different types of red bus to be found. The London motorbus fleet in 1958 was solidly diesel-powered but over the past decade London has been pioneering the use of alternative methods of propulsion, first with diesel-electric hybrids, then hydrogen fuel cell buses and most recently full electric buses. So much so that hybrids represent roundly half of the London

double-deck fleet – and the number is growing. There have been hybrid single-deckers in London but there were none at the time of writing; there is, though, a growing fleet of full electric single-deckers, plus a dozen hydrogen buses.

And in Central London it is difficult to ignore the distinctive New Routemasters built by Wrightbus. There are 999 full-size versions, 11.3m long, and one shorter 10.2m version. Eight years ago, we were out searching for the prototypes on route 38, and then the low-numbered examples on the 24 – some still carrying London registration marks before the LTZ marks took over. Although some of the more novel aspects of the New Routemasters have disappeared – the conductor, the open third door for hop-on-hop-off passengers – these quirky buses are still eye-catching and while no other operators are queuing to buy some for themselves they have influenced the styling of mainstream double-deckers like London Sovereign's six Volvo SRMs and ADL's Enviro 400H City models.

Back in 1958 nine out of every ten London buses were double-deckers, but today it's barely seven out of ten, reflecting the increased use of single-deckers. Alexander Dennis tops the list of suppliers, accounting for just over half of all buses, with 80 per cent of all single-deckers and 40 per cent of double-deckers. Volvo supplied 33 per cent of London's double-deck fleet, but no single-deckers. Wrightbus comes third with over 16 per cent of the total fleet, comprising the 1,000 New Routemasters as well as double-deck integrals and StreetLite single-deckers.

By far the majority of the single-deck fleet is made up of ADL Enviro200 variants. These are direct successors to the hugely popular Plaxton Pointer Darts – the affordable pioneering low-floor buses that many operators favoured. The Dart family has revolutionised the London single-deck fleet with around 2,000 in use as this is written. But within the Dart/E200 fleet there are many variations. The current E200 version ranges from 9.0m long with one door and seats for up to 26 passengers to 10.9m long, two doors and 31 passengers.

The Wrightbus StreetLite is popular in some London fleets, mainly in the DF (door forward) version, but it has a long way to go to catch up with the Enviro200. Like its ADL rival, it is available in different lengths – from 25-seat two-door 9.7m to 31-seat two-door 10.8m. And the WF (wheel forward) version is in use in single door 28-seat 8.8m guise.

Optare has sold several of its models into London fleets from the familiar Solo, in versions from 7.8m to 9.6m long, to the larger MetroCity, from 9.9m to 10.6m long, to the even larger Versa, from 10.4m to 11.1m long, to the 12m Tempo. Arriva and RATP have 10.6m MetroCity electric buses.

As this is written some once familiar bus types are fast disappearing. The Dennis Dart/Plaxton Pointer was once a single-deck staple in London as it was throughout the UK, but by the time you read this there are likely to be fewer than 100 still in TfL service. Another Dennis product, the Trident/Alexander ALX400 may well be extinct by this time as might the last Plaxton President double-deck bodies.

A few years ago, I started to plan these day trips to discover what different delights lurked in places beyond the centre. Sadly, TfL no longer issues printed bus maps but all praise to Mike Harris (www.busmap.co.uk) for his historic and current bus maps produced in the 1970s London Transport style. My choice of destination was random – open the map, look for places with an obvious concentration of buses, and head there during one of my London visits. And I have rarely been disappointed.

Some of these places I know well – Kingston and Croydon are often revisited. Kingston can produce variety such as Mercedes-Benz Citaro Ks, unusual Optare Olympus-bodied Tridents, Optare Versas, the rare combination of Volvo B9TL and ADL Enviro400 bodywork, and occasional sightings of

The unusual combination of Volvo B5LH and ADL Enviro400 bodywork is found in the London fleets of Arriva and Stagecoach. This 2015 10.5m Stagecoach example passing Elephant & Castle tube station in May 2016 is crossing a newly installed cycle lane.

LONDON BUS TYPES

1958

Single-deck

AEC Regal
AEC Regal IV
AEC Regal IV BEA
Guy Special GS
Leyland Tiger

Double-deck

AEC Regent RT
AEC Regent RLH
Leyland Titan RTL
Leyland Titan RTW

2019

Single-deck

ADL E200/E20D
BYD D9UR**
Irizar i2e**
Mercedes-Benz Citaro
Optare MetroCity
Optare MetroCity**
Optare Solo
Optare Tempo
Optare Versa
Van Hool A330FC***
VDL SB200***
Wrightbus StreetLite

Double-deck

ADL Trident/E40D
ADL E40H*
AEC Routemaster
BYD K10**
Scania N94UD
Scania N230UD
Volvo B5LH*
Volvo B5TL
Volvo B9TL
Wrightbus Gemini 2DL
Wrightbus New
Routemaster*
Wrightbus StreetDeck*

| * Hybrid |
| ** Electric |
| *** Hydrogen fuel cell |

ABOVE: *Metroline received eight BYD K10 electric 10.2m double-deckers in 2016 and this one is seen in Maida Vale in February 2017. It has just 54 seats.*

RIGHT: *A small fleet of eight 11.9m hydrogen fuel cell single-deckers arrived between 2010 and 2013. These are VDL SB200s with Wrightbus Pulsar 2 bodies and this 2010 example is seen near the Tower of London in May 2018, operated by Tower Transit.*

RIGHT: *Go-Ahead was the first London fleet to specify Egyptian-built MCV eVoSeti bodies on Volvo B5LH chassis. This 10.5m example is at Elephant & Castle in May 2016 when just a few weeks old.*

the still-rare Wrightbus StreetDeck. RATP London United buses dominate the Kingston scene, many of them Scania OmniCity double-deckers, some dating back to 2008. Go-Ahead and Stagecoach are the other major operators of these Polish-built buses. And Croydon has yielded former Metrobus Scania double-deckers and Arriva currently runs a batch of rare Optare MetroCity electric single-deckers.

There are suburban centres where you can simply stand and marvel at the sheer quantity of buses serving the area and hope to discover something a bit different. Golders Green is one of these places – a constant flow of red buses interrupted by white National Express coaches at this important pick-up/set-down stop. Another is Ealing, which on a Sunday was a revelation. Where many UK town centres are quiet on a Sunday, with a restricted bus service, Ealing was benefiting from high-frequency services. Another rewarding Sunday was spent around the Elephant & Castle area, where I first encountered

the MCV eVoSeti Volvos and realised that some of Stagecoach's ADL Enviro400s were on Volvo B5LH chassis, an unusual combination.

Venturing east, Stratford is a multi-modal feast with the busy bus station feeding and being fed by main line and Jubilee Line trains. Further east, the busy centre of Ilford is served by some of the relatively rare Wrightbus StreetLite WF.

And north to Walthamstow with the usual suspects plus the three ADL Enviro400VE (virtual electric, using charging pads at termini) double-deckers. To the west, Harrow is well worth the trip. As are Hounslow, right under a Heathrow flight path, and Richmond with its delightful Thames-side setting. Closer to Central London, Putney High Street and Putney Bridge offer a constant stream of red buses with good photo opportunities on the bridge.

The background machine that is TfL usually guarantees consistent standards across its patch. Although the printed maps may have gone, the online and at-stop information is excellent, and while double-deckers with two doors and as few as 21 seats on the lower deck may seem odd to those of us in the rest of the UK, we are always told that London is 'different', even 'special', and that could be why we still find London's bus scene so interesting. At least there is much more for us to see than the 4,460 near-identical buses of 60 years ago, efficient as they doubtless were.

The first batch of BYD D9UR electric single-deckers with 12m-long ADL Enviro200EV bodies went to Go-Ahead in 2016 for the Red Arrow 507 and 521 routes. One approaches Waterloo Bridge in April 2017.

From minis to midis

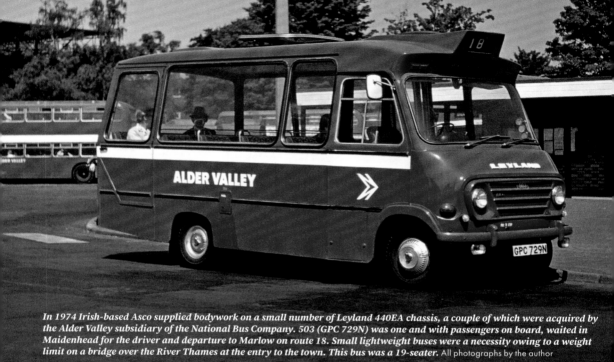

In 1974 Irish-based Asco supplied bodywork on a small number of Leyland 440EA chassis, a couple of which were acquired by the Alder Valley subsidiary of the National Bus Company. 503 (GPC 729N) was one and with passengers on board, waited in Maidenhead for the driver and departure to Marlow on route 18. Small lightweight buses were a necessity owing to a weight limit on a bridge over the River Thames at the entry to the town. This bus was a 19-seater. All photographs by the author

Tony Wilson looks at the variety to be found among small buses over the years.

The years after the 1970s witnessed one of the many periods of change within the history of the bus since the days of the stage coach (two words, small 's'); the term defined as a covered vehicle pulled by horses that carried people and goods on regular routes.

It was during this period the likes of that well-known busman Harry Blundred changed the face of the bus as we then knew it and revolutionised the industry. This came in the shape of the minibus, a small creature capable of seating up to 16 passengers in what were converted van-derived vehicles.

Like an advertising campaign of the time for a popular alcoholic libation, these buses were able to reach parts others could not reach, places such as housing estates and small back roads in towns and cities. They could also venture further afield to the highways and byways of the countryside, able to provide links to hamlets and villages previously unconnected to the route network.

However, as time progressed the popularity of these buses grew, such that more would be necessary to cope with increased headways, or something larger was required. It was the latter that won the day and 'little' became 'large,' with the production of purpose-built buses with up to around 30 or 35 seats, plus a small number of standees.

Thus, the midibus was created by firms such as Dennis, Mercedes-Benz, MCW and Optare, not van conversions but vehicles built in their own right.

The following collection of pictures illustrates some of the models that helped to change and define the face of bus travel during those interesting years.

ABOVE: *December 1975 and eight Alexander-bodied Ford A0609 23-seater midibuses were supplied to the West Midlands PTE. As fleet numbers 4730-37 they were based at the Acocks Green garage and employed on a new Dial-A-Bus network in the Dorridge area. 4734 (JOV 734P) is seen here during that long sizzling summer of '76.*

BELOW: *When the Leeds-based Roe bus body building plant closed in September 1984, several former employees and the plant manager formed the Optare company in February 1985. One of their first projects was new bodywork for a batch of 13 Dennis Dominos that were supplied to the South Yorkshire PTE as numbers 41-44 and 46-54. 53 (C53 HDT), here some seven years into its revenue-earning life at the Sheffield Interchange during September 1992, is in Little Nipper livery.*

ABOVE: *A rare combination of bodywork and chassis was provided by Wadham Stringer and Bristol with this LHS6L supplied to the Harvey bus company based in Cornwall, who ran the bus service between Penzance and Mousehole under their trading name of Blue Bus. Small buses were required owing to narrow roads, particularly at the Mousehole end of the route. Configured as a 35-seater and acquired new in 1981, by September 1988 it along with an ECW-bodied version, had been acquired on takeover by the Western National bus company and became number 1565 (KRL 444W) in that fleet. The tiny Western National fleet number is carried below the offside windscreen.*

LEFT: *While Optare was engaged on producing bodies for the SYPTE Dennis Dominos, a further 15 bodies were on the production line for the West Yorkshire PTE. This batch was built on Leyland Cub chassis, with fleet numbers 1801-15. All were 33-seaters but the first four were supplied with dual-purpose seats. However, their time with WYPTE was brief and at least two migrated south to Cedarbus of Sussex. What was 1805 (C805 KBT) became Cedarbus number 5 and is shown here in Worthing during a very wet October 1986.*

ABOVE: *During late 1989 an innovative-looking 8.5m-long bus was supplied on demonstration to London Buses. This was a 28-seater Carlyle-bodied Dennis Dart registered G349 GCK, which spent its first few months trawling round several London bus garages. In January 1990 it moved into Edgware garage and was used on route 251 (Arnos Grove to Edgware). Here it passes along Lawrence Street, Mill Hill bound for Edgware Station in the following February. Whilst a route number was able to be shown in the destination box, roller blinds for the rest were not, so a purpose prepared blind display was affixed inside the lower windscreen. By the end of 1990 London Buses had acquired the bus and allocated it fleet number DT168, the last in a substantial number of the type, which paved the way for many more Darts of varying body styles to operate within the London area over the following years.*

ABOVE: *1985 saw the appearance of the CityPacer, a purpose built 25-seater bus from Optare. Built on a Volkswagen LT55 chassis, 11 were acquired by the Welwyn-Hatfield Line during August 1987 as fleet numbers VO1-11 and placed into service on a small network of new services between the two Hertfordshire towns. VO5 (E514 PWR) is seen in Welwyn Garden City soon after delivery.*

ABOVE: *It's June 2002 and on a Monday Bakewell market day, Clowes Coaches of Longnor had this 30-seat Wright Consort-bodied Leyland DAF 9-13R in service on the irregular extension of route 458. Normally running between Longnor and Hanley, it was extended on one Monday a month to and from Bakewell. Here registered ELZ 2972 it was originally registered F599 OYX when it was new in 1988.*

ABOVE: *Like the Optare CityPacer the Metrorider from Birmingham based MCW was a purpose-built midibus launched at the 1986 Motor Show. The model soon became popular with many companies up and down the country but only had a three-year production life with MCW before the project taken over by Optare. Before that though a number were acquired in late 1987 by Northumbria Motor Services in north-east England. However, several soon after delivery were transferred south and placed on hire to a couple of companies in the London area. Harrow Buses, a new low-cost subsidiary of London Buses based at Harrow Weald Garage, acquired a couple, which included 824 (E824 BTN), seen here in Headstone Lane in August 1988 as it operated over the H12 route between Stanmore Station and South Harrow Station, complete with roundel and a large 'BUS' motif to signify its London Regional Transport contracted credentials.*

ABOVE: **To service London Regional Transport contracts in west London, the CentreWest subsidiary of London Buses acquired a fleet of 17 Mercedes-Benz 26-seat Wright bodied midibuses. Whilst most featured a snub-nosed bonnet area to cover the engine, one stood out from the rest. MW17 (LDZ 9017) had a sloping design to cover the engine, here as it passed along Swakeleys Road, Ickenham bound for Uxbridge on route U1 from Ruislip during April 1993.**

LEFT: **Whilst three axles were not necessarily associated with such small vehicles, Peugeot produced the Talbot Pullman in that format. Generally used for council-sponsored social transport, the low design provided good access at the rear for less able-bodied users and passengers in wheelchairs. Kentish Bus acquired 16 of this design during 1989-90, for a network of routes in the North Kent area under the Kentish Hopper banner. However, now and again one or two escaped and headed for the city such as 881 (G881 SKE) in April 1990, in Victoria on National Express route 706 from the Tunbridge Wells area.**

ABOVE: *The first of two examples from Hampshire-based Wadham Stringer of Waterlooville. The company produced bodywork for both ambulances and buses and entered the midibus market with a small number of demonstrators on Dennis Dart chassis. In July 1991 a 35-seated model named the Portsdown appeared and having done the rounds was acquired by Midland Red North where it became 526 (J556 GTP). It enters Wolverhampton bus station in May 1998, with the destination already set for a return journey to Cannock on route 870.*

TOP: *Production of the Duple body for the Dennis Dart was taken over by Carlyle when the Duple business closed. Other builders soon joined in, most notably Reeve Burgess, and later Plaxton, with the Pointer. Two Carlyle-bodied Darts later received rebuilt front ends using the Pointer design and found new work on the streets of Stratford-upon-Avon with the Stratford Blue company. Originally London Buses DT137 (H137 MOB), this one became Stratford Blue 698 (ANZ 8798) and was caught in the bright May sunshine of 2004.*

MIDDLE: *Another day another tri-axle. One of the oddest looking modern midibuses of the day was a fleet of TBP Freeway-bodied Peugeot Boxers supplied to the Pathfinder company based in Newark. Operated under the Shuttleco banner, 24 (N985 XCT) arrives in Newark in May 1996 on route S2 from Nottingham. The company was later taken over by Nottingham City Transport.*

BOTTOM: *The second example from Wadham Stringer was a more upright and austere-looking coach - note the high floor level - named the Winchester and built in late 1993. Six years on in 1999 it was in the hands of Arriva North Midlands. There it was numbered 809 (L766 DPE) and assigned to the limited-stop X38 (Burton-on-Trent and Derby), here on arrival in the latter city being driven with vigour on approach to the bus station.*

ABOVE: *In the late 1990s Marshalls of Cambridge produced a new bus in the shape of the Marshall Minibus as a competitor to the successful Dennis Dart. One of the type, P980 PTM, was supplied to Hatfield based Universitybus. The company provided a network of routes throughout Hertfordshire for the public as well as their own staff and students, to serve the various locations of the university. This single bus though spent most of its revenue-earning career on local cross-town route HA1 in Harpenden, where it passes through the verdant centre in November 1996.*

BELOW: *Looking particularly European was one of three Neoplan N4009 midibuses supplied to Merseytravel during spring 1995. These followed on from an earlier batch of similar but larger buses. 7032 (M302 YBG) is in St John Street in Liverpool city centre in July 1997. Despite its appearance the bus only sat 17 passengers. It was used mainly on the inner city 222 route.*

Reeve Burgess, a small firm based at Pilsley, near Chesterfield in Derbyshire, produced a body named Beaver. Initially an upright looking design, it was placed on chassis from the likes of Dodge, Iveco and Mercedes-Benz. Demand outgrew the company's facilities and was subsequently taken over by Plaxton at its Scarborough premises. The Beaver model was updated and became popular with many bus companies up and down mainland Britain. It also found favour amongst the big three of Arriva, First and Stagecoach, as well as small and not-so-small independents. One such was Trent which took several batches of the model including Mercedes-Benz Vario 280 (R280 RAU), here on a local section of route R61 between Matlock and Wirksworth in the early 2000s.

ABOVE: *When Reg's of Hertford bought a Dennis Mini Pointer Dart in 2002 it took advantage of changes to Britain's vehicle registration system with the introduction of the numerical year identifier. Two area letters preceded the year number 51 for the latter part of 2001 and early 2002, thus creating an almost perfect registration for the company as BU51 REG, which could be read as BUS 1 for REG. The vehicle is hard at work in May 2003 in Hertford as it operated one way around the houses of the Pinehurst Estate on the cross-town route 333.*

BELOW: *This look at the world of the midibus is rounded up with a rare type to find in Britain. In April 2004 this stranger passed through Cambridge city centre on a contracted service to and from the Oakington immigration reception centre. It was a Spanish Castrosua Carsa-bodied Scania N94UB registered YP52 CUU and operated by the Kent based King's Ferry company.*

Four decades in Chester

Bus operations in Chester have changed significantly over the last forty years.
Cliff Beeton takes a look.

I n 1980 bus services in Chester were regulated under the licensing regime set in place by the 1930 Road Traffic Act and were provided by two main operators, National Bus Company subsidiary Crosville Motor Services which operated interurban services from adjacent towns and villages, and Chester City Transport which ran the local services within the city boundary. At that time there were still restrictions on Crosville picking up and setting down local passengers within the city unless they were travelling to or from destinations beyond the boundary.

Both operators were still running their last few half-cab double-deckers. Crosville's were Bristol Lodekkas, mainly on services D1 and D2 to Llangollen and Oswestry, operated from Wrexham

ABOVE: *Chester City Transport Guy Arab V 42 (XFM 42G), was the last Arab to operate in normal service with the operator and is seen outside the Cathedral on a 10 to Grove Avenue in February 1982.*

ABOVE: *Crosville had the largest fleet of Seddon buses outside Scotland, owning 100. It was the only NBC subsidiary to operate them. SPG800 (OFM 800K) is seen in the city centre on the C42 to Plas Newton in all-over green livery without the white relief band in March 1982.*

LEFT: *Some of last Crosville Bristol Lodekkas working into Chester were on the D1 and D2 to Llangollen and Oswestry, operated by Wrexham garage. DFG168 (CFM 903C) is seen reversing off the stand at Delamere Street bus station in April 1981. It would be withdrawn that summer.*

BELOW: *Crosville acquired many second-hand Bristol VRTs and Daimler Fleetlines in 1981 to replace the remaining Bristol Lodekkas and speed up the conversion to 100 per cent one-man operation. Bristol VRT DVG546 (UUF 113J) is a recent arrival from Southdown and is outside Liverpool Road depot on a C53 to Kingsway in July 1982. It had been new in 1971.*

garage. Chester City Transport had four Northern Counties-bodied Guy Arabs left, and these included DFM 347H, the last Guy bus built for the home market, in 1969. The Lodekkas would finish in the summer of 1981 with the final Guy Arab in normal service lasting until 1982.

At that time most of the Crosville services and National Express coaches used the bus station in Delamere Street. Chester City Transport buses used on-street stops, particularly around the Cathedral. Delamere Street bus station would close at the end of the 1980s, being replaced by a new one at Northgate Street. At the same time the on-street stops by the Cathedral were abolished, with all services concentrated on the new bus station.

The Crosville fleet in Chester at the start of the 1980s contained the standard NBC Bristol VRTs, Leyland Nationals and Leyland Leopard coaches, but other interesting vehicles included some early dual-door Leyland Nationals, Seddon Pennine RU buses with dual-door bodies and bus seats, as well as dual-purpose single-door examples introduced in 1973. Also resident was the unique mid-engined Seddon Pennine VII ex-demonstrator, UBU 72N.

All photographs by the author.

ECW coach-bodied Bristol REs and Leyland Leopards demoted to bus work could also appear.

The main Crosville central works was situated locally at Sealand Road, and this undertook repairs on the whole fleet as well as occasional work for other NBC companies.

In the early 1980s following on from the last Bristol VRTs, standard ECW-bodied Leyland Olympians and Leyland Tiger coaches started arriving as well as second-hand Bristol VRTs with ECW bodywork from Southdown and with East Lancs bodies from South Yorkshire PTE. Daimler Fleetlines with ECW bodies also arrived from Southdown. Many of these second-hand buses were sourced to help replace the last Lodekkas and to complete the conversion to 100 per cent one-man operation.

Chester City Transport on the other hand followed on from its last Guy Arabs in 1969 with regular orders for Daimler Fleetlines and later Leyland Fleetlines, all with Northern Counties bodywork. When the Fleetline was discontinued, Chester turned to the Dennis Dominator, again with Northern Counties bodywork. These continued to be purchased until four Northern Counties-bodied Leyland Olympians arrived in 1984 followed by

another pair in 1989; these would turn out to be the last new double-deckers purchased by the company. Batches of Dodge minibuses with Northern Counties bodywork followed.

As newer buses arrived some of the older Fleetlines were converted to part open-top to operate city sightseeing tours, in competition with Guide Friday which had started running open-top tours in the city.

Mainly a double-deck fleet, Chester also had small batches of Leyland Leopards bodied by Northern Counties and Duple. In 1983 it acquired three Marshall-bodied single deck Dennis Dominators from Merthyr Tydfil Transport.

With deregulation looming in 1986 big changes were on the horizon. Chester City Council formed the arm's length company Chester City Transport Ltd in October 1986 to take over the buses. For Crosville the Secretary of State for Transport decreed that the company would be split in two in preparation for deregulation and a future sale, with separate English and Welsh companies, both working into Chester. The Welsh company would adopt a white and green livery with the fleet name Crosville Cymru, with its English counterpart

RIGHT: *Chester always operated single-deck buses, but at one time they represented only a small proportion of the fleet. Northern Counties-bodied Leyland Leopard 70 (NMB 70P) waits outside the Cathedral on a 4 to Canal Bridge in May 1983. New in 1976 it was a short PSU4C/2R with Pneumocyclic gearbox.*

BELOW RIGHT: *Wrights of Wrexham started running competing services against Crosville Wales on the Chester to Wrexham route after deregulation. DAF Optare Delta H512 YCX was one of two bought new by the company and is seen leaving Chester bus station for Wrexham in June 1993 with a rival Crosville Wales VRT behind.*

BELOW: *Under Drawlane ownership Crosville Wales took examples of the East Lancs Greenway. SNG882 (IIL 4822), which started life as London Country Leyland National LPB 180P, is seen picking up in the city centre on a 1 for Wrexham in June 1993.*

retaining the Crosville brand and adopting a new dark green and orange livery, with the orange soon being replaced by cream. The last new vehicles for Crosville before the enforced split were a batch of six coach-seated Leyland Olympians for the 70-mile-long X1 Cymru Coastliner from Chester to Caernarfon in a bright green and white livery with a large red dragon on the side.

Crosville was sold to ATL Holdings in March 1988, while Crosville Cymru was sold to a management buyout, later passing on to National Express and then Drawlane. Drawlane would also purchase Crosville from ATL in 1989 bringing the two Crosville companies under common ownership. Drawlane also owned East Lancashire Coachbuilders, which was rebuilding Leyland Nationals as the National Greenway, examples of which would later arrive at Crosville Wales. A batch of East Lancs-bodied Dennis Dominators were ordered for Crosville for use on the Wirral peninsula and in Chester. Drawlane would later became British Bus.

Deregulation on 26 October 1986 would see Chester City Transport and the two Crosville companies come under attack from new and old-established operators taking advantage of the abolition of road service licensing. Some bus services were registered commercially with no subsidy; others which were not registered as commercial but were deemed socially necessary were subsidised by the council by means of competitive tendering. Crosville and the new Crosville Wales operation suffered particularly hard here, as smaller businesses with lower operating costs won tenders to provide services that the two larger companies had not registered commercially. This included not only complete routes, but also early morning, evening and Sunday journeys on some routes that the bigger companies still operated during the day. This caused problems for passengers as return tickets were generally not transferable between operators. The restriction prohibiting Crosville from picking up and setting down passengers within the city boundary was abolished at this time.

Wrights of Wrexham started running into Chester from Wrexham in competition with Crosville Wales using Leyland Nationals, DAF/Optare Deltas, Leyland Lynxes and ex-Greater Manchester PTE Leyland Titans. But despite running modern buses that were smartly-presented it closed in 1993.

Devaway was started in 1987 by two ex-Crosville employees and over the years operated many Leyland Nationals before being sold to Arriva Cymru in 1998. Ex-West Riding National PWW 716R is seen loading for Kinnerton in June 1993. It dated from 1976.

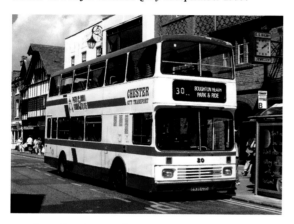

Loftys of Bridge Trafford ran an assortment of elderly Leyland Leopards on the C36 into Chester from Ince and Elton. It later went on to purchase brand-new Mercedes minibuses for this and other contracted services. Local coach operator Huxleys of Threapwood used Ford coaches and later Leyland Nationals on route C83 to Wrexham. Merediths of Malpas also used Ford coaches on its C58 to Whitchurch. These were all former Crosville routes.

Two ex-Crosville employees formed Devaway in August 1987 to operate council tenders and commercial routes into Chester. Devaway started with second-hand East Lancs-bodied Bristol REs from Halton Transport, whose red and cream livery was adopted by their new owner. Later arrivals included Leyland Nationals and Bristol VRTs, as well as rare Wadham Stringer-bodied Ward Dalesmans from Darlington Transport. Devaway later returned to Halton to buy Mark 2 Nationals and Leyland Lynxes. The end for Devaway came in March 1998 when it was sold to Arriva Cymru, the successor to the British Bus-owned Crosville Wales business.

Not all new visitors to Chester were small companies. MTL, the former Merseyside PTE operator, began running on the Birkenhead to Chester corridor. In the 1970s the C1-C5 services from Chester to Birkenhead via different routes had been some of Crosville's most profitable. MTL would become part of one of the big groups in February 2000 when it, too, was purchased by Arriva.

After Drawlane purchased Crosville from ATL in 1989 the future looked more promising, but this was to prove short-lived as Drawlane started to divide the company up and allocate it piecemeal to neighbouring subsidiaries Midland Red, Bee Line and North Western. Midland Red buses would now appear in Chester from Crewe on the C84, and North Western from Northwich and Warrington. The remaining parts of Crosville at Chester along with those at Birkenhead and Ellesmere Port were sold to Potteries Motor Traction in February 1990 along with the freehold depots. Initially the cream and green livery was kept, but gradually the fleet was repainted into the red and yellow PMT livery but with Crosville fleet names, after initially opting for a green and yellow version of the PMT livery. Vehicle exchanges also occurred, so it was now possible for PMT vehicles to appear in service at Chester. The Dennis Dominators ordered by Drawlane for Crosville on the Wirral peninsula were subsequently delivered to Midland Red at Crewe and would become regular visitors to Chester on the C84.

New vehicles to arrive under PMT ownership were Mercedes minibuses with PMT's home-built bodywork as well as MCW Metroriders and later some of the first Dennis Darts with Plaxton Pointer bodywork. These proved popular with passengers and further follow-on batches arrived including low-floor examples. When PMT became part of Badgerline in 1995 some buses appeared with a badger motif behind the rear wheels.

Badgerline later merged with GRT to form FirstBus. After initially allowing subsidiary companies to keep their own liveries, FirstBus introduced a standard livery when the pink, purple and off-white FirstGroup 'Barbie' scheme was introduced from 1997. This would make vehicle transfers between subsidiaries easier as repaints would no longer be needed.

Apart from a few delivered new in the Chester park-and-ride livery, all new buses for Crosville would now be standard FirstGroup-liveried Wright-bodied Scanias and Volvos, with many second-hand examples also arriving from other FirstGroup companies as declining profits cut back spending on new vehicles. The Crosville name would later disappear altogether as the operation was rebranded as First Chester and Wirral.

In 1997 British Bus, owner of Crosville Wales, merged with the Cowie group to become Arriva. British Bus had always let subsidiary companies choose their own individual liveries, but Arriva immediately introduced a mandatory nationwide cream and aquamarine livery. The predominance of East Lancs bodywork on new vehicles also ceased. The first new vehicles to appear in the new livery in Chester were a batch of Northern Counties-bodied Volvo Olympians branded for route 1, Wrexham to Chester.

Both Arriva and First vehicles working on the Chester to North Wales corridor were relaunched in 1999 under the Lynxx brand with buses wearing a purple, cream and buff livery. On some buses the purple was later replaced by indigo.

In 2002 First Chester and Wirral imported some

Chester City Transport acquired many youthful second-hand buses to supplement those bought new. One such purchase was 11 (F882 VSJ), an all-Leyland built Olympian new to A1 Service member McKinnon of Kilmarnock and seen here at the bus station in February 2000 on a 1E to Rhuddland Road.

Only 36 examples of the Marshall Minibus were produced, with Chester purchasing two new and obtaining some second-hand examples from London General. 249 (P149 LMA), bought new in 1996, is loading at the bus station on a 23 to Marbury Road in September 2001.

RIGHT: *First Chester and Wirral Dennis Dart 40100 (L934 HFA) is seen working service 9 to Pipers Ash which was a former Chester City Transport route in March 2008. The Plaxton-bodied bus had been new to PMT in 1993.*

American Blue Bird school buses, for which an outstation was opened at Wrexham. They were regulars in Chester as they received maintenance there. They wore school bus yellow livery rather than First corporate colours.

Chester City Transport meanwhile started to buy Dennis Darts, initially with Reeve Burgess and later Plaxton Pointer bodywork. Low-floor examples later arrived with Marshall bodies followed by two rare Marshall Minibuses in 1996. Chester also embarked on a policy of buying youthful second-hand buses. This made things interesting for enthusiasts, but probably indicated that declining profits could no longer justify brand-new vehicles being purchased every year.

Second-hand Dennis Dominators arrived from Brighton, Hyndburn and AA Buses. Leyland Olympians came from Derby, A1 Service and West Yorkshire PTE with a mixture of Leyland, Roe and East Lancs bodywork. A batch of rare Leyland Lions from Clydeside Scottish also arrived, along with some equally rare Marshall Minibuses from London General to join the pair purchased new. Changes over the decade gradually saw the Chester livery change to a larger proportion of cream and less brown than previously.

Larger low-floor buses purchased new were six Wright Access Ultralow-bodied Scania L113s for park-and-ride work, painted in a red, blue and white livery, followed by eight BMC Falcons, also for the park-and-ride operation. The Falcons would prove to be the last new buses ordered by the company. Chester City Transport came under sustained competition in 1996 when the South Lancs minibus operation was started and competed on many of its routes with second-hand minibuses in a dark green and cream livery, similar to the post-NBC Crosville scheme.

A rebranding exercise in April 2005 saw Chester City Transport become ChesterBus with the livery being altered to cream, yellow and blue. Previously the blue had been used to indicate a low floor bus.

Declining profits saw the council put ChesterBus up for sale in July 2006, but things went far from smoothly. Arriva stepped in and registered many of the ChesterBus routes itself, to start running in January 2007. ChesterBus then went to the High Court alleging anti-competitive actions, but its case was eventually thrown out.

A surprise move in June 2007 saw ChesterBus sold to First Chester and Wirral. The only buses involved in the sale were the Marshall-bodied Dennis Dart SLFs and the open-top Leyland Olympians that operated the City Sightseeing Tour. The rest of the fleet was available for First to use at a peppercorn rent until replacement vehicles were drafted in from other FirstGroup subsidiaries. The ChesterBus depot was not included in the deal.

After the sale went through Arriva and First were running against each other on some of the ChesterBus routes, leading to complaints to Cheshire County Council about over-bussing and congestion at bus stops and in the bus station. The council brokered a quality partnership deal between First and Arriva on route 1 between the City Centre and Blacon, with a joint timetable and interavailabile tickets. It was marketed as The Blacon Pointer. This had the desired effect and things returned to normal once again. Following complaints about the age and condition of the First vehicles operating the quality partnership it was agreed to replace some of the older Scanias with a batch of two-year-old Volvo B7RLEs from First West Yorkshire to bring them up to a similar age to the Arriva vehicles.

In 2009 First introduced 14 new Wright Eclipse Urban-bodied Volvo B7RLEs, some of which were for the Chester park-and-ride in a new blue, white and orange livery. Reorganisation within FirstGroup in 2010 would see First Chester and Wirral, which had been under the control of First Potteries since PMT purchased the remains of Crosville from Drawlane in 1990, now come under the control of First Manchester at Oldham.

In 2012 FirstGroup started selling off subsidiary companies that were not performing to the required standard and said that the Chester and Wirral operation would be put up for sale. After months of speculation it was announced that Stagecoach was the successful purchaser and would take over operations from 13 January 2013. All First staff transferred to Stagecoach along with 110 buses, and the depots at Liverpool Road, Chester; New Chester Road, Rock Ferry and the outstation for school buses at Wrexham.

Initially the buses received Stagecoach fleet names and fleet numbers on their First livery. These were applied overnight on 12-13 January, ready for service the following morning. Stagecoach had also transferred some new Enviro200s and youthful Dennis Darts into Chester to start running from the first day. Repaints then commenced on buses that were being kept long term, but many of the older buses, including the Marshall-bodied Dart SLFs which First had acquired with the ChesterBus operation and most of the early Wright-bodied Scanias would be soon replaced with newer vehicles. Surprisingly four of the

ABOVE LEFT: *Alexander-bodied Scania N113 31113 (H636 VNW) was transferred into Chester from First West Yorkshire to operate ex-ChesterBus routes. It is seen working a 1A to Blacon in March 2008. This bus had been new to Yorkshire Rider in 1991.*

LEFT: *The only buses transferred to First Chester and Wirral when it purchased ChesterBus were the seven Marshall-bodied Dennis Dart SLFs, including 40172 (V372 KLG) on former ChesterBus route 5 to Huntington in June 2009, repainted in full First livery.*

ABOVE: *The buses of Helms of Eastham have been a regular sight in Chester for many years, working several services including the shuttle from the station to the city centre. One of Helms' more unusual buses was East Lancs-bodied Leyland Lion F389 GVO seen in June 2009 on a school service. The bus was new to Nottingham City Transport in 1989 and the body was built to NCT's specification.*

RIGHT: *Avon Buses of Prenton was a regular visitor to Chester on the Neston and West Kirby routes using modern buses, many purchased new like MCV Evolution-bodied Dennis Dart 108 (AE08 DKO) seen in February 2013 on a 25 to West Kirby. Avon Buses suddenly ceased trading in October 2018.*

earlier Wright-bodied Scanias did however receive Stagecoach livery. Some of the Blue Bird school buses at Wrexham were repainted from yellow into Stagecoach livery too. The Leyland Olympian open-toppers were later replaced with converted ex-Stagecoach London Dennis Tridents.

Arriva chose its Chester-Wrexham route 1 to launch its first Sapphire service in April 2013. Nine Alexander Dennis Enviro400 double-deckers that had been made surplus by new hybrids at Birkenhead were fully refurbished with leather seats and free Wi-Fi as well as charging points. Best Impressions designed a new two-tone blue livery for the buses which were also given select J-ABW (Arriva Buses Wales) registrations.

Arriva cut back the 84 Crewe to Chester from

half-hourly to hourly in January 2016, prompting Routemaster Buses of Crewe to introduce an hourly C84 to replace the withdrawn journeys. Routemaster Buses already ran into Chester once a week on the 83 from Nantwich via Bunbury on Tuesdays. GHA Coaches, which ran the 82 into Chester from Northwich and ran into Chester on other routes from North Wales, objected to this, and registered an identical route running five minutes ahead of the Routemaster journeys. Despite having purchased four Wright Pulsar Gemini buses from Ensign, the Essex-based dealer, to work the C84, Routemaster suddenly stopped running the route in March 2016 and later ceased trading. Unfortunately for GHA, they succumbed to the same fate in July 2016. The demise of Routemaster Buses would see D&G Bus take over the Tuesday-only service 83 to Chester, and later the 82 from Northwich from Arriva which had run it on tender since the demise of GHA.

Stagecoach later converted the Chester to Ellesmere Port and Birkenhead services to their Gold Standard, with brand-new Enviro300s in a gold and brown livery with leather seats and Wi-Fi. New Enviro200 MMC buses were ordered for the Chester park-and-ride in 2017 in a new livery. The 2009 Volvo B7RLE Wright Eclipses that they replaced were repainted into standard fleet livery and later transferred to Lincolnshire.

Such was the success of Arriva's first Sapphire route between Chester and Wrexham that a decision was taken to invest in 13 new Alexander Dennis Enviro400 City buses in 2017 to upgrade the route. These wore a modified Sapphire livery of silver, light blue and dark blue.

Over the years since deregulation the number of independents running into Chester has gradually fallen. A casualty in 2018 was Avon Buses of Prenton, running into the city from Neston and West Kirby for many years with a smart fleet of buses, many having been purchased new. Stagecoach stepped in to continue running the routes. Helms of Eastham still runs into Chester and now operates the shuttle service from Chester Railway Station to the city centre.

Stagecoach closed the ex-First depot in Liverpool Road in February 2018, selling the site for student accommodation. The buses were relocated to a site at the old Waverton railway station, some five miles south of Chester.

At the time of writing in early 2019, some six years after the sale to Stagecoach, there are now no ex-First Chester and Wirral vehicles left in the area. The 09-plate Volvo Eclipses were transferred to Lincolnshire in 2017 while the remainder have been withdrawn and replaced with newer vehicles. Two ex-First Manchester Volvo B9 Wright Eclipse Gemini double-deckers were transferred to Chester in 2018. These originated at Wigan but were soon transferred within Stagecoach to Scotland, later returning to Merseyside at Gillmoss.

LEFT: *Arriva North West took delivery of ten MAN EcoCity 18.240 buses in 2013 with support from the government's Green Bus Fund. 5007 (MX13 AAY) is in Chester bus station on an X30 to Warrington, one of its regular routes, in February 2013.*

Freshly repainted in Stagecoach livery in February 2013, 28553 (YN05 WKK) is an ex-First Wright Solar-bodied Scania L94. It is about to work a 2 to Liverpool, some 20 miles to the north.

Using the public

Love or loath them, without them, there would be no need for buses. Chris Drew illustrates how members of the public can fit in to bus photographs.

BELOW: *What can one say about Imberbus? It's quite unique. It's not an open day at a garage, or a preservation meet. It's not a running day in the usual sense of the word because there's no home for it to run from. And what, I hear you say, about the buses? They all have their origins in London at least 100 miles away and apart from a few modern oddments that make an appearance, they are all Routemasters, original ones. I must own up to the feeling that usually my heart drops when I arrive at a rally/open day/road run and see enough Routemasters to stock a medium-sized garage. But Imberbus is different. I think it's just because of the Routemasters that it works so well. Then there is the reason for them being in the middle of Salisbury Plain. It's the village of Imber of course. The village was taken over by the Ministry of Defence for training purposes at the time of the second world war and today is still used to show soldiers how to fight house-to-house warfare. It does make one wonder if there was a bus service to the village before the area was requisitioned. If so, was the service ever frequent enough to meet head-to-head like these two did. I was lucky to be on the spot to see the whole scene unfold before me. I stood transfixed as the next best thing to a committee was formed and, as if by magic, the problem was solved. There were a few 'mmmms,' the odd scratch of the forelock and a 'well I never' to fill in the gaps while decisions were made, small things like that always work wonders.*

ABOVE: *People who stand in front of you! Believe it or not, the public can be a pain in the posterior at times, there I've said it. That's it out of the way. I'm sure, though, I'm not the only bus photographer who's been in places where other like-minded picture takers have been quite vocal about their feelings towards them, but ... who was going to tell this lot where to go? With age sometimes comes wisdom and, with luck, patience. It was a sunny day and I was quite happy to wait awhile to get the shot ... then it struck me, they are the shot. How often does a story like this appear in front of my camera? Around me voices murmured with disapproval or made loud tutting noises or even the odd slightly less that discreet cough. Along the barrier cameras were poised. A thought went through my head that if they do all go off together, the sound of thirty shutters at the same time would be deafening, the equivalent of the bus paparazzi. I pulled out of the group and left them to it, I thought I had my shot.*

ABOVE: *The slipway at Broadway Street near the Sally Line port was a rudimentary affair. A hut for a ticket office and what was the draughtiest corner of Portsmouth to park your vehicle. There were two coaches parked on the slipway ready for boarding. I made my excuses, grabbed my old Agfa Isolette and managed to get this shot, my first with a ferry. I was helped by the fact that most of the passengers had to disembark the coach because of fears of grounding on the steep angles between the slipway and the ferry ramp. Only the infirm could stay on board while the driver gingerly inched towards the ferry. It was MED 270F, a Leyland Leopard with Duple Commander 51-seat bodywork belonging to Shadwell's of Warrington. I rushed back to the family steed and we boarded, parking near the rear ... err, stern. It was then that it struck me that the ferry was not much more that a Viking long boat without any oars. The sails had been replaced by a garden shed on stilts in which the driver stood. There were no comforts for the passengers, so the hardier members found their way to the bow and stood there, looking for all the world like the Port Isaac's Fishermen's Friends about to burst forth into a shanty.*

ABOVE: *This is real affection and attention to detail. Having just traversed a circuit of Amberley museum and out of a special pocket came the destination blind key which was used to extricate stones from the tyre. As most of the journey around the site was on chippings, this was going to be an ongoing job all day, but it made sense because stones can damage a tyre or paintwork when they come lose. It also shows that it's the small everyday things that bring a scene to life, putting the cherry on the top of the cake. The hundreds of man hours spent on the fabric of a bus like Wigan Leyland Titan PD2 number 140 would be just that without a crew in uniform to add authenticity for the adults and an air of magic for the younger generation.*

BELOW *The theory of six degrees of separation states that because we are all joined together by chains of acquaintances, you are just six introductions away from any other person on the planet. Or, it could be describing the row of photographers that can be seen at the entrance to many a gathering of buses. This time was in 2011 when the Cobham running day was moved to Dunsfold aerodrome. Returning to the original theory, I expect that there are several acquaintances in the photograph that are slightly less than six degrees away from whoever is reading this.*

ABOVE: *Knowing what you want from a photograph is one thing but when luck steps in to lend a hand, you feel privileged indeed. The bus entered the scene in central Derby, stopping in exactly the position I was hoping it would. On other occasions, this might have been enough, but ... a procession of strangers moved into the vista from stage left. My first instinct was to curse my luck but as they set foot onto the crossing, my eye was drawn to the subject I was taking, and I hit the shutter release before it was too late. There is a definite feeling of regret when the shot passes before you've had time for the brain to catch up. Then there was the wait before I could confirm if I had made the correct decision. Not then the instant gratification of the digital cameras of today, but even now, if the moment's gone ... it's gone. But the bollard, that's another story.*

BELOW: *A couple of Paris Renaults on the left bank - but of the Thames rather than the Seine. This was Victoria Embankment in London in the late 1970s, so it would be worth a 5p bet that one of the drivers would be Robert Jowitt, and so it was ... I win.*

ABOVE: *I came across this scene at the top of Reigate Hill on a warm summer day in 1982. It instantly sent my memory back to 1966 when the British Broadcasting Corporation was about to go colour on BBC2. All the previous year there had been television test transmissions using 625 lines as opposed to the 405 used by the other two - yes two - channels. Some of the films were documentaries but others were fine pieces of art. One reminded me of this scene. It was set in or near a French petrol station in the back of beyond. There were no words spoken but it was not a mime. Various characters pass by with their stories, one being a stereotypical English family in a Morris 1000 who have a puncture and while 'Father' changes the wheel, 'Mother' sets up a full-blown picnic on the kerb side with Janet and John, all very prim and proper, just like the couple here. The coach itself was London Country DL14, a Duple-bodied Leopard all decked out in colours for the 747 airport service. I wonder if the people got their flight.*

LEFT: *To call what happened in Northern Ireland in the last half of the 20th century, 'the troubles' is much akin to saying the Gulf War was a bit of a fracas. It shouldn't have been much of a surprise when what was happening in Northern Ireland daily spilt over the sea to the UK mainland and especially to London ... big city ... lots of soft targets. The targets were not only prominent buildings, areas and pubs known to be connected to the armed forces, but also places like Harrods, the Ideal Home Exhibition, (in a litter bin next to an escalator) and in the lobby of the Hilton Hotel. In many, but not all, cases a telephone warning was given and identified by a code word. Sometimes the times or the locations were wrong leaving little or no leeway to evacuate an area. Then there were the hoax calls which were sent just to cause as much disruption as possible. This was just such an occasion. The scene was enacted dozens of times in the 1970s and 1980s. This was in fact the summer of 1986, a normal lunchtime with Whitehall full of tourists and workers. It might have been an unattended suitcase found in Trafalgar Square or indeed nothing at all, just a malicious phone call: we were never told. I came out of my office to find Whitehall converted into an open-air bus garage, engines stopped, waiting. Other vehicles were being diverted elsewhere.*

Twice the lens, half the cab

This Park Royal-bodied AEC Renown, which originally carried East Yorkshire Motor Services' dark blue livery, then the short-lived NBC blue, dates from 1965, and was photographed in the Promenade, Bridlington in August 1977. It lasted another two years after this. All photographs by the author.

The urge to capture disappearing half-cab double-deckers spurred Peter Rowlands into bus photography in the late 1970s. His original camera was less than ideal, but forty years on he celebrates its overlooked benefits

Like many of us, I suspect, I started my bus photography with a camera that was less than ideal for the purpose. In my case it was a Yashica twin-lens reflex with a non-interchangeable standard lens.

It had been a remarkably generous present from my parents for my fourteenth birthday, and it was more than acceptable. Admittedly, its large, box-like shape was uncool, and you had to look downwards into the viewfinder, rather than straight ahead, which could make alignment difficult; but under the right conditions it could take stunning photographs. I wasn't one to look a gift horse in the mouth.

It was only when I started photographing buses in earnest 12 years later that the Yashica's drawbacks really hit me. I'd been tempted into the pursuit by the realisation that half-cab double-deckers would soon vanish from the streets. There were still hundreds in service up and down the country – some barely ten years old, others much more venerable – but they wouldn't be around much longer. One-person operation was the future, and they simply weren't built for it.

I travelled a lot for my work, and realised I had the chance to photograph these buses while they were still around, along with any others that took my fancy. I assumed my trusty Yashica would do the job, but I hadn't reckoned on the problems I would encounter with it.

A particular issue was the lack of zoom capability. As I soon learned, this was a significant impediment. When you're photographing buses in the wild, other objects frequently get in the way – pedestrians, traffic, street furniture. With a zoom lens you can pull the bus forward or push it back in the image and take the shot at the ideal moment. Without one, you're hobbled.

This meant that I tended to photograph buses when they were quite close to me, or else I took the shot when they were too far away to occupy their rightful proportion of the frame.

In fairness, prior to about 1960 zoom lenses were a great rarity in still photography, yet people managed to take admirable bus photographs despite this – mostly using either a standard lens or a telephoto lens. But for me, taking opportunist bus pictures with limited time, the flexibility of a zoom lens would have been invaluable.

Another constraint was that I only got twelve shots on a roll of 120 film, whereas I could have had two or three times that number on 35mm film. If the film ran out at a critical moment, I had to fumble the camera out of its awkward leather case, remove and seal the exposed film, carefully insert a new one and wind it forward to the right point, then put the camera back in its case. How many perfect

ABOVE: *A West Midlands PTE Metro-Cammell-bodied Guy Arab is seen in Birmingham in June 1977, when it was 27 years old. It is believed to have been the longest-running of Birmingham City Transport's large fleet of buses with "tin fronts." It was also one of the first buses ever photographed by the author. It has been preserved in Birmingham's former dark blue and cream livery.*

BELOW: *Preston Corporation favoured forward-entrance double-deckers in the 1960s. This Metro-Cammell-bodied Leyland PD3 was delivered in 1961, and is seen 17 years later, in July 1978. Behind it is a Pennine-bodied Leyland Panther dating from 1972.*

pictures did I miss while I was doing all that? (I should have ditched the case, but I had a sense that the heavy and ungainly camera would have been too vulnerable without it.)

Photographing buses up close also brought another problem: parallax. The Yashica's standard 80mm lens was the equivalent of a 50mm lens in a single-lens reflex, yet with large objects like buses, it might as well have been wide-angle. It gave a surprisingly acute perspective, and if I tilted the camera upwards, background objects such as buildings and lampposts tended to "lean in" from the sides, producing crazy verticals that weren't vertical at all.

Yet if I took the picture while the bus was still

LEFT: *Seen in Leicester in May 1978 is one of the council's last 20-strong batch of Metro-Cammell-bodied Leyland PD3s, delivered in 1967. After withdrawal it saw brief service with Stagecoach in Scotland. Behind it is the last of a batch of five unusual short-wheelbase two-door Bristol RESL single-deckers, which were delivered in the same year, then sold to Blackburn Borough Transport in 1978.*

RIGHT: *Still looking in incredibly good shape in June 1977, this Weymann-bodied London Transport RT dates to 1951. It is seen on London's North Circular Road, having recently been transferred to Palmers Green depot. It was withdrawn late the following year, aged 27.*

Two Leyland Titans in Blackpool in July 1978 – a 1964 Massey-bodied PD2A in the Fylde Borough Transport fleet (since preserved) and a 1968 Metro-Cammell-bodied PD3A from Blackpool Transport. These were somewhat lost in the centre of the original print.

distant, I got acres of empty road space in front of it and endless swathes of buildings in the background, and there was no guarantee that the bus itself would be sharp or clear enough.

A definite upside of the camera was its 120-film format. The area of those square images was massive – three and a half times that of 35mm film. This mean that relatively speaking, my pictures had a very dense grain with lots of detail: ideal in theory for enlargement or reproduction in print.

Sadly, the reality was somewhat different. I always used colour negative film, and when photographic shops developed colour films back in the 1970s, they provided sets of "enprints" – a portmanteau word meaning "enlarged prints".

Typically, these were three and a half inches square: about two thirds the size of a 35mm enprint. From much bigger negatives I got far smaller prints. It seemed absurd, but it was a reality I had to live with.

TOP RIGHT: *Photographed in Burton in September 1978, this Massey-bodied Daimler CCG5 of East Staffordshire District Council was new to Burton Corporation in June 1964. The bus operation lasted only another six years, then was one of the earliest in the wave of council bus fleet disposals that followed.*

BELOW: *A rear-entrance Bristol Lodekka FS6G of Hants & Dorset dating from 1965 passes Southampton's sprawling civic centre in June 1979. The complex was opened in stages between 1932 and 1939 and is grade II listed.*

ABOVE: *An ECW-bodied LD-series Bristol Lodekka of Eastern Scottish is seen near Waverley Station, Edinburgh, in September 1977, when it was seventeen years old.*

At the time, the limitations of the result were a disappointment rather than a genuine problem; but ten years later, when I started submitting articles and pictures to the bus press, they became a real frustration.

Back then, reproducing images for publication from negative film meant presenting photographic prints for scanning by the publisher. However, I was all too aware that many of my diminutive enprints looked distinctly unpromising and might be rejected. For a start, the main subject (the bus) was often too far away. Then there was the question of the colours; some of those old prints were faded or had acquired a mysterious cast.

To make matters worse, many had been badly printed in the first place. Photographic shops were particularly poor at processing dull-weather photographs taken on fast film to compensate for low light; the prints often came out looking much too dark, even though all the detail was plainly present in the negative.

ABOVE: *Looking tired after fifteen years' service, this Midland Red (BMMO)-built D9 is seen in Leicester in May 1978, eighteen months before its withdrawal. It worked in Leicestershire all its life and is now in the hands of Leicester Transport Heritage Trust, where it has been undergoing restoration.*

To compound the problem further, back in the 1970s photographic shops often turned out prints on fancy paper with names such as "pearlescent" and "silk" (this had a tangible silk texture embossed in the surface). These finishes, I learned later, played havoc with scanning – hiding detail, and even making the image look blurred when the negative wasn't.

ABOVE LEFT: *Council-owned Northampton Transport had a reputation for keeping an immaculate fleet, as this May 1979 picture of a Roe-bodied Daimler CVG6 shows. Dating from 1968, the bus was one of the final five Daimler half-cab buses built for the home market. The very last one was preserved and is now with Northampton Transport Heritage.*

ABOVE RIGHT: *This Hartlepool 1961 Roe-bodied Leyland PD2/40 was originally owned by West Hartlepool Corporation Transport until a redrawing of the municipal boundaries in 1967 saw the merger of West Hartlepool with Hartlepool. It is seen on a dull July day in 1978, followed by a Bristol RE.*

Sometimes I had enlargements made and submitted those for publication instead, but it was an expensive business, costing several pounds per enlargement in today's money; and bear in mind that I was submitting each image speculatively. Some of the enlargements might be rejected by the magazine, but I still had to pay for them.

So, I tended to self-edit, and avoided submitting old 120-format pictures for reproduction at all unless the colours were sparkling and the bus looked big enough in the enprint to impress.

It was only in the early 2000s that I finally found a way round some of the drawbacks of those early bus pictures. Like many fellow photographers, I bought a flatbed scanner, and when I wanted to submit images for publication I scanned the prints myself. At least now I had control over the cropping, the colour balance and the brightness.

However, the old 120 enprints were very small and often flawed, and the scans sometimes failed to yield detail that I knew was in the negatives. Editing the results in Photoshop sometimes took a

BELOW: *This 1964-built AEC Regent V of Cardiff Corporation was bodied by Neepsend, a short-lived sister-company of East Lancashire Coachbuilders under the ownership of its then parent, Cravens of Sheffield. It followed an order for similar East Lancs-bodied models. It was photographed in June 1977.*

THE TWIN-LENS REFLEX: AN ALTERNATIVE TAKE

Whereas a single-lens reflex camera (SLR) uses the same lens for view-finding as for taking the picture, a twin-lens reflex (TLR) has a separate lens for each function, one mounted above the other. This eliminates the need the for the prism and flip-up mirror found in SLRs, simplifying the mechanics.

The image from the upper viewfinder lens is reflected into a horizontal ground-glass viewing screen on top of the camera, which is shaded in use by a flip-up cowl. There's a magnifying lens so you can optionally lift the camera to your eye. Because there's no corrective prism, the image is reversed in the viewfinder. It's like seeing the subject in a mirror.

Classic TLRs used a large film format called 120. This produced square negatives or transparencies measuring 56mm by 56mm. In the day, the format was always referred to as "two and a quarter square," meaning inches. Nowadays it is often called "medium format." By contrast, 35-millimetre frames were two thirds the width and just forty per cent of the height.

TLRs tended to be favoured by portrait and landscape photographers. Zooming was not what they were about, and in fact more or less all of them had fixed focal-length lenses. Several makers including Rollei and Mamiya (the big guns of the format) did provide lens extenders that gave some flexibility, and Mamiya offered models with fully interchangeable lenses; but zoom lenses were nowhere to be found.

RIGHT: *The contradiction: small square prints were supplied by photographic shops from large 120 negatives, whereas much larger prints were supplied from far smaller 35mm negatives. The true potential of the upper picture can be seen in the version on page 50 which was scanned from the negative. The lower picture of a London Routemaster, included for comparison of the negative and print sizes, was taken in Seven Sisters Road, Tottenham in July 1987.*

ABOVE: *The upper lens of the Yashica handled focusing, while the lower one was for taking the pictures.*

LEFT: *This simulation shows the camera's top cowl in the raised position, revealing the viewfinder with its reversed rendering of the subject. It looks like an LCD screen, but it's just ground glass showing a reflected optical image thrown up by the mirror beneath it. The circular magnifying glass could be flipped horizontal to allow the camera to be brought up to eye level.*

ABOVE: *Close cropping of an originally square image has brought this East Lancs-bodied AEC Regent V of Southampton Transport to centre stage in the frame. It was built in 1966 and was photographed in June 1979.*

very long time, and still didn't always to justice to the original.

You might ask why I didn't scan the negatives rather than the prints: a very reasonable question. Partly it was because I'd separated them from the prints and stored them inaccessibly. There was also the small matter that I didn't have a scanner that could do the job. More fool me.

Eventually, in 2019, I treated myself to a scanner that could handle film as well as prints, and at the same time I retrieved those 120 negatives from storage.

Wow! Suddenly I had a cornucopia of potentially reproducible bus pictures from the 1970s. Forty-year-old images that I had only ever seen in those modest-looking square enprints were revealed in their glowing colours at last, often with stunning depth and clarity.

So, what happened to my twin-lens reflex? Well, I finally replaced it with a single-lens reflex in the early 1980s. Having a zoom lens was a joy and a revelation, and I quickly realised it was only perverse loyalty to the Yashica that had held me back. I'd knew forfeited the enormous negative area of the twin-lens reflex, but the benefits of the SLR more than compensated. There was no way I was ever going back.

Yet if I'd made the move sooner, I wouldn't have a remarkable resource of 120 negatives from the 1970s to play with forty years later.

On these pages you can see some of the results.

BELOW: *Delivered to Aldershot & District in green livery in 1965, this Weymann-bodied Dennis Loline is seen in Guildford in February 1979 in the ownership of NBC's Alder Valley subsidiary. Judicious brightening has brought life to what could have been a drab shot.*

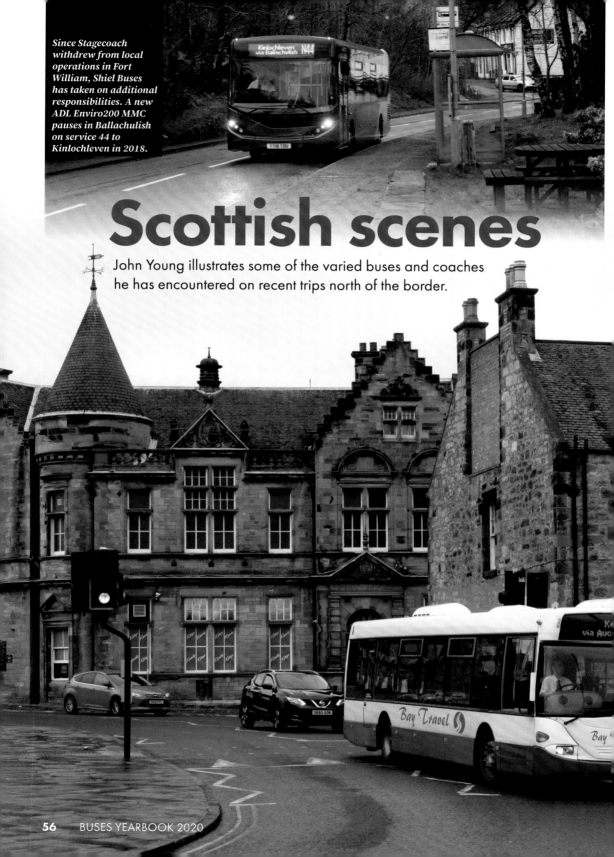

Since Stagecoach withdrew from local operations in Fort William, Shiel Buses has taken on additional responsibilities. A new ADL Enviro200 MMC pauses in Ballachulish on service 44 to Kinlochleven in 2018.

Scottish scenes

John Young illustrates some of the varied buses and coaches he has encountered on recent trips north of the border.

This Volvo B10M with Alexander (Belfast) body was new to Ulsterbus in September 1994. Its high capacity - 65 seats - makes it ideal for school duties, on which it was still working for Dodds of Troon when captured in Ayr in April 2018, 24 years later.

BELOW: *This Scania OmniCity CN94UB was new to Menzies, Heathrow. Working for Bay Travel of Cowdenbeath in 2017, YN53 GGO is arriving in Kirkcaldy on service 18 from Kelty via Auchtertool.*

ABOVE: *JMB Travel of Newmains provides several services in the former Central Scottish area. SN53 AVO, a former Lothian TransBus Pointer Dart SLF, passes through Wishaw.*

ABOVE: *McCall's Coaches of Lochmaben operates several contracted services for Dumfries and Galloway Council. An Optare Solo SR in the livery of the SWestrans regional transport partnership arrives at Gretna Outlet Village on a service 382 journey from Lockerbie. Stagecoach-operated journeys on the 382 continue south to Carlisle.*

ABOVE: *Stagecoach 54238 is numerically the last of a batch of eight Volvo B11RT with Plaxton Elite i bodies for Coastliner service X7 from Perth to Aberdeen. The journey via Dundee, Arbroath, Montrose and Stonehaven takes a little under four hours and operates hourly, seven days a week. Here it loads at the main stop in Perth in the summer of 2018.*

ABOVE: *Several Van Hool Astromegas new to Stagecoach in 2009 for the Oxford Tube service between Oxford and London were cascaded to Stagecoach West Scotland for service X77, which links Ayr with Glasgow using the M77 motorway and A77 trunk road. They were re-registered with appropriate numbers; this is X77 SCJ.*

Rennies Coaches of Cowdenbeath has retained its separate identity despite being a long-established part of Stagecoach. A cascaded and re-registered Volvo B7R with Plaxton Profile body is seen in the Scottish capital in June 2018. The Volvo had been new to United Counties in 2006 as KX56 JZN but is now 866 PYC. Only the Stagecoach fleet number barely visible below the windscreen, 53275, gives a clue that Rennies is part of a multi-faceted transport group.

Although based in England, at Berwick-upon-Tweed, Borders Buses is owned by Craig of Campbeltown and most of its services are in Scotland. Optare Versa YJ13 HHY pauses at Milfield with a service 267 journey from Berwick to Wooler via Etal and Ford. The Versa is a 49-seater and was new to Weavaway of Newbury in 2013. Borders Buses came in to being in 2017 following the acquisition by Craig of Berwick-based Perryman's Buses

ABOVE: *In 2018 Stagecoach West Scotland applied Western SMT heritage livery to 28689 (VCS 376) with Western-style fleet number KC689 indicating Kilmarnock depot and Scania chassis. The bus is a K230UB with ADL Enviro300 body and was new in 2014. It turns in to Ayr bus station at journey's end, after a two-hour run from Glasgow via Newton Mearns, Kilmarnock and Prestwick Airport.*

ABOVE LEFT: *Stagecoach East Scotland repainted three buses in commemorative liveries in 2018 to celebrate 100 years of Dunfermline depot. The double-deck variant is seen on an ADL Enviro400 arriving in to Dunfermline on service 19A, a route more usually operated by modern single-deckers. The livery is of a style used in the late 1980s by Scottish Bus Group subsidiary Fife Scottish Omnibuses.*

LEFT: *Irvine Cross was once a hotbed of activity and interest for the bus enthusiast with buses from the fleets of AA, A1 Service and Western Scottish evident. Nowadays traffic levels have reduced, but it is still a busy hub. The former A1 trunk route between Ardrossan and Kilmarnock, now numbered 11, has seen four batches of new stock since coming under Stagecoach control in 1995. The most recent is illustrated here with a route-branded ADL Enviro400 MMC loading for Kilmarnock. The lengthy Clyde Coaster service 585, Greenock to Ayr, also passes through, along with several more local services.*

LEFT: **Borders Buses use a mixture of vehicles on the X95 linking Edinburgh with Carlisle via the Borders towns. The X95, previously operated by First, was a rail replacement service, although the railway has now reopened between Edinburgh and Galashiels. Most journeys only operate a portion of the route, either Edinburgh to Hawick, or Galashiels to Carlisle. The full trip takes three and a half hours. Here a Caetano Levante-bodied Volvo B9R, new in 2011 to Selwyn's of Runcorn for National Express duties, pauses at Canonbie, near to the English border.**

LEFT: **This Volvo B5TL with 79-seat Wrightbus Eclipse Gemini 3 body is further proof, were it needed, of Lothian's commitment to quality and exacting standards of fleet presentation. It loads at Leith on a beautifully sunny day in September 2017.**

BELOW: **This impressive Scania/Irizar i6 in the fleet of West Coast Motors is performing a Scottish Citylink journey on the 915 from Uig, on the Isle of Skye, to Glasgow. Providing a valuable link to the outside world and onward travel opportunities, it pauses for a customer to board in Ballachulish. There are still three hours to go of the eight-hour trip.**

ABOVE: *Lothian has upgraded and expanded its fleet significantly in recent times, to meet air quality targets and to compete against First. Looking at home in the fleet, this Volvo B9TL with Wrightbus body is notable for being one of 50 acquired from London and extensively refurbished and re-registered with Northern Ireland LXZ-series numbers. Most of the Volvos came from Metroline but this bus was one of two which were new to Tower Transit.*

ABOVE LEFT: *It's New Year's Eve 2018 in Oban, as a West Coast Motors ADL Enviro200 works the cross-town service from Dunollie to Soroba, a 17-minute ride. The bus was new to TLC Travel of Bradford in 2012.*

LEFT: *Fifteen Scania OmniCity double-deckers delivered in 2006-07 were unusual vehicles to find in service with Lothian Buses and were originally in a blue-based livery for the Airlink service to Edinburgh Airport. 999 (SK06 AHN) is seen in 2017 after being downgraded to bus operation. It was the highest-numbered bus in the fleet until the numbering from 1001 upwards of the ex-London Volvos acquired in 2018.*

An adventure in Thailand

Inveterate bus rider Bob Hind samples the challenges of bus travel in Thailand.

Unplanned and hatless

There are plenty of more intrepid explorers than me, who will advise you how to approach travelling by bus in Thailand and, I must confess, for six of the seven days I was in that country, I resisted the urge to sample the local transport mostly through ignorance but partly through the fear of getting totally lost. I like to plan my trips and that was not going to be possible without a firm grasp of the native language.

Hua Hin lies about 150 miles south of Bangkok on the western coast of the Gulf of Thailand. It is a small city of about 80,000 inhabitants distributed along a 12-mile strip of its main thoroughfare, Highway 4. There are many and various routes from the centre into the hinterland and a 20-minute frequency service on the three-and-a-half-hour route to and from the capital. But the local bus routes in and around Hua Hin appeared to be provided by just four services, the principal one travelling up and down Highway 4 every ten minutes between the airport in the north and Khao Takiab (Monkey Mountain) in the south. This Green route conveniently passed my hotel, so I had some confidence in the existence of the service, as I had seen it regularly. The other three routes (Red, Orange and White) appeared to be widening circles to the west of the city centre.

These are provided by *Songthaew* pronounced 'song tao' but the locals do use the word bus! They are a variety of Nissan, Isuzu and Toyota trucks supporting a covered cabin housing two rows of benches. *Songthaew* means 'two rows' in Thai. So, the accommodation seats eight to ten passengers (12 at a squeeze) and as many standees as can cram inside or hang from the open back. The vehicles are hailed anywhere (there are some bus stops for longer distance routes) and equally stopped anywhere using a shrill bell. Fares are generally 10 to 20 Thai Baht (about 25p to 50p) depending on distance and are paid to the driver when alighting.

This entire process, hail-and-ride potentially stopping every 20 yards, and the total honesty of walking round to the driver's cab means that, while

LEFT: *Who needs free Wi-Fi and wood-effect floors? The basic interior of a Songathaew.* All photographs by the author.

BELOW: *The Songthaews are pick-up trucks with the load bed adapted to carry passengers. Two Green route Songthaews in central Hua Hin. Nearest the camera is an Isuzu with a Toyota alongside.*

ABOVE: *The country buses are based on light truck chassis and offer a higher standard of comfort than the Songthaews.*

RIGHT: *A Green route Nissan Songthaew passes a bus shelter with the silhouette of a reclining figure on the wall behind the bench.*

BELOW: *The Hua Hin Songthaew route plan.*

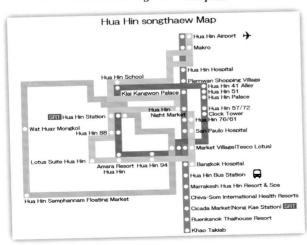

departures from each end of the route are regular, the actual journey time can vary enormously, so it is not surprising that one previous visitor described the service as 'not very punctual'.

I am on the roadside at 08.20, equipped with a schematic map of the four routes, which I found on the internet. No timetables except an indication of when each route starts and finishes and its supposed frequency. I am standing next to a parking sign that has bus stop on it, just in case, but I need not have worried as my first attempt at hailing works. My hotel is at the southern end of the Green route, so I am aiming initially for the airport. The bus is not busy, although people come and go throughout the journey, so I manage to get a seat.

Within 13 minutes we are in the centre where several *Songthaew* are parked amongst cars and a couple of more conventional and ancient red buses are waiting to head out of town. We wait a couple of minutes then continue north, calling into the grounds of Hua Hin hospital. Despite enjoying a seat, a breeze blows through the cab and a gust catches my baseball cap which disappears under the following traffic. Not only am I unsure where I am going, I now face a day out in temperatures in the upper 90s without any protection on my head. The face of a young man sitting opposite sympathises without speaking. I wonder if this venture is a good idea. We reach the airport at 08.54, but we don't go in. The bus swings across the dual carriageway, drops us on an overgrown verge and quickly draws away.

On the way, I had looked out for an Orange route bus which, the map showed, finishes at Makro near the airport, but I had not seen one. So, then I start to question the frequency, 06.00 to 22.00 that I had found on website compared to another site that says 18.00 to 21.00. To complicate matters, today is Vesak Day which, because of the full moon, combines the celebrations of the Buddha's birthday, with his enlightenment and his death. This means there is much activity at the various temples, but does it also mean that the 'not very punctual' network will be even more problematic? I opt for safety and hail the next Green route bus, that appears ten minutes later, and return to the centre.

Waiting with the Royals

One of the many attractions in Hua Hin is the railway station and, despite my aversion to rail travel, I am curious, as the location of the King's Klai Kangwon summer palace in Hua Hin prompted the building of a royal waiting room at the railway station, and the guidebooks say it should be seen. The Victorian-style station, originally built in 1910, was rebuilt in 1925. In 1967 the Sanam Chandra Palace was moved to the station to become the Sanam Chandra Palace Railway Pavilion, exclusively for visiting royalty. It is quaint and packed with Thai tourists who eagerly await the arrival of the next elderly (three classes) diesel train, to take a selfie! In fact, the arrival and departure of the train does nothing to disperse the crowd, who continue to photograph everything from every angle.

My next *Songthaew* route starts from the railway station and is the only one of the four routes that ventures away from the centre into more rural parts. It has two purposes: to visit the Floating Market and Wat Huay Mongkol Temple. The information, gleaned from the internet, suggests

A Red Songthaew which turned out to be masquerading as a tuk tuk. It is based on a Chinese Kingstar Jupiter light pick-up.

that it runs hourly, leaving the station on the hour, so I am hoping for a 10.00 departure. The only thing is, it doesn't leave from the station; a previous explorer advises newcomers to look for the 7Up sign and the stop is close by!

He's right; a white board propped up against a tree shows three departures at 10.00, 12.20 and 14.20 (hardly hourly) but I am more assured when a young Thai woman joins me in anticipation of the first journey. At about 10.10 she shows some concern and asks me, in perfect English, how long have I been waiting. There is a phone number on the board which she decides to call. After a very calm conversation, she informs me that there is no 10.00, the next bus is midday. I naively ask what happened to the 10.00 and she tells me, quite casually, that the driver had to visit his temple. That is the most original reason for non-operation I have ever come across; she leaves, and I ponder how to fill the next couple of hours.

I walk back to the main street and am surprised to see a silver *Songthaew* on what I thought would be the Red route. However, feeling adventurous, I hop on and when we reach the centre the driver comes around and asks me where I am going. I say, 'the bus station', as I have noticed one on the Red

route, and he looks blank. A conversation ensues with the only other passenger who eventually says, 'the minibus station'. I nod, the driver smiles, and we set off.

Kidnapped by tuk tuk

The minibus station is a hive of activity as it seems to be the centre for a fleet of Toyota minibuses destined for all parts away from Hua Hin. Attendants on a platform in front of the ticket office call out a destination, passengers flock to a 20-seater and depart. I watch with amusement although the chaos does appear to work. A red *Songthaew* is parked at the front of the station and I assume I can return to the railway station. I ask the driver if he is heading there and with much gesticulation, he invites me to sit in the cab with him. As we set off he says 'tuk tuk' at which point I realise the branded bus is operating as a taxi and I am about to be charged £2.50 instead of 25p for the short journey. The driver, pleased with his capture, tries to persuade me to do a sightseeing tour but he accepts that I am adamant and that I only want the railway station.

At 11.45 I am reunited with the young Thai woman and three newcomers (all Thai) who have joined us. The nearby street vendors offer shade from the midday heat and the hope that we might buy something, but we are all pleased to see our bus pull up just after noon. A conversation between my companions and the driver appears to end to everyone's satisfaction and I ask my new friend how long the journey will take and when we should expect to arrive back at the railway station.

She answers, somewhat evasively, that we go to the Temple first. We set off at 12.05 and are soon enjoying a windy dash through the suburbs and into greener scenery, although the street vendors still border the road for as far as the eye can see. After about 25 minutes, we arrive at Wat Huay Mongkol, about nine miles west of Hua Hin, below a towering 12m-tall black Buddha amid crowds of visitors and worshipers. I appear to be the only westerner here. My companions disperse, the Thai lady tells me we are staying here for an hour and the driver invites me, in broken English, to view the sights.

Slightly bewildered, I wander round the site where shops sell food, drink and every Buddhist effigy ever conceived. The huge statue is one of Thailand's most famous monks, Luang Phor Thuad, who, 400 years ago, was credited with many miracles including regularly turning salt water into drinking water. A very practical miracle in these temperatures.

I find, in the near distance, an even bigger golden statue so this does seem to be a religious site of some significance. However, I remain in ignorance. When my companions return, the driver asks if we want to shop at the Floating Market and I anticipate being stranded for another hour. However, there seems little enthusiasm for the suggestion, so he sets off at some speed and gives us a circular tour of the Floating Market, several small shops surrounding a sizeable lake and circled by a miniature railway. We arrive back in Hua Hin just after 2 o'clock. I alight at Market Village. What I thought would be a local 20-minute trip has taken two hours.

The heat and humidity hit again once we have lost the cool breeze blowing through the *Songthaew*, so I opt to return to the safety of the Green route and to experience the southern end of the route. It seems much busier now and there appear to be more Green buses, so it is not long before I am headed, past my hotel, towards Monkey Mountain.

The hail-and-ride concept continues to intrigue me but works quite smoothly. Fifteen minutes later we are at the terminus where another half dozen *Songthaews* are parked up. I can't fathom how this all works, whether there is any form of frequency or is it just the chaotic situation it appears?

An elderly lady with a shopping trolley joins me for my return to my hotel. She just manages to lift her trolley on to the standing platform and sits, on the adjacent seat, clinging to the handle. A few minutes later she struggles to stand, and I pass her trolley down to her on the roadside. Her gratitude, in an alien language, is a humbling finish to my adventure. The *Songthaews* work for all ages and, even if I was daunted by the prospect, the locals made pleasant travelling companions.

This was the most ill-prepared trip I have ever ventured on and I still have no idea what had happened to the Orange and Red routes that were on my map. But the experience was such a contrast to the overly regulated system we suffer at home that it was quite an enjoyable day and I didn't really mind being kidnapped by a tuk tuk driver and being given an unexpected taste of commercial Buddhism.

BELOW: *A Songthaew in central Hua Hin. Note it is fitted with different wheels front and rear.*

Island hopping

Mark Bailey looks at the varied types of buses which have served the islands around the British mainland

iving on an island, even one the size of mainland Britain, has always held a fascination for me, possibly because I've always lived on the coast and constantly been exposed to the effects of the sea in all its various moods. It seems to me the smaller the island the more its geography affects day-to-day life, in particular the transport links to, from and across the island, where tide times and weather conditions can often restrict accessibility and dictate schedules.

The following photographs taken over the last forty years or so illustrate a variety of buses and coaches found on some of the smaller islands that make up the British Isles. The journey starts in the far south west on the Isles of Scilly and continues up the Irish Sea in a clockwise direction around Britain, ending a few miles off the coast of France in the Channel Islands.

ABOVE: *St Mary's, Isles of Scilly The Isles of Scilly are a collection of small islands lying 28 miles off Land's End in Cornwall. The largest of them is St Mary's and from mid-March to October a ferry service provides a link to Penzance. For many years Vic's Tours of Hugh Town ran island tours and pictured in August 1984 fully laden near Old Town is FDL 842, a Duple Vista-bodied Bedford OB, new in 1949 to an Isle of Wight operator, Pearce's Tours of Ryde. The coach survives in Norfolk and has been immortalised as a 1:50 scale die-cast model by Corgi.*

RIGHT: *Holyhead, Holy Island Despite its remote location in north-west Wales, Holy Island benefits from good road and rail links to Anglesey and beyond due to the significant freight and passenger traffic that utilises the shortest ferry route between Britain and the Irish Republic, Holyhead to Dun Laoghaire. Arriva Cymru succeeded Crosville as the dominant bus operator, but several independents also provide local services. Seen in Holyhead in April 1999 is S91 UEY, a Plaxton Beaver-bodied Mercedes-Benz Vario of Jones of Llanfaethlu, loading on service 25 to Aberffraw on Anglesey.*

Douglas, Isle of Man *The Isle of Man lies in the Irish Sea between England, Northern Ireland, Scotland and Wales, to which views of each can be seen on a bright day from the summit of Snaefell. There is an airport at Ronaldsway and daily ferry services link the capital, Douglas, with Liverpool and Heysham. Douglas Corporation operated buses in the town for 55 years until the formation by the Manx Government of Isle of Man National Transport in October 1976. Pictured between workings in August 1976 is 66 (KMN 837), a Northern Counties-bodied AEC Regent III.*

LEFT: *Ramsey, Isle of Man* **The other constituent in the formation of Isle of Man National Transport in 1976 was Isle of Man Road Services, which operated the remaining network of routes across the island to Ramsey, Peel, Castletown, Port Erin and Port St Mary. In 2009 the trading name was changed to Bus Vannin, as shown on Optare Spectra-bodied DAF DB250 41 (MAN 41H) at Ramsey in September 2010 which had just returned on service 20A from Andreas.**

BELOW: *Millport, Great Cumbrae* **The small island of Great Cumbrae sits in the Firth of Clyde, accessed from the Scottish mainland by a ferry service from Largs. Millport is the only town, home to the Cathedral of the Isles, and linked to the ferry slip by route 320. Pictured in August 2006 departing the bus terminus in Millport is Ikarus Citibus-bodied DAF SB220 W235 CDN of Cumbrae Coaches.**

ABOVE LEFT: *Rothesay, Bute* **Firth of Clyde neighbour Bute has a ferry service connecting the island's capital town of Rothesay to the mainland at Wemyss Bay, and there is also a short ferry crossing across the Kyles of Bute to the Cowal peninsula. Once, services were operated by Stagecoach subsidiary Western Buses but by the time of this August 2006 photograph the network had been taken over by West Coast Motors. Smartly-liveried YJ05 PWU, a Wrightbus Cadet-bodied VDL SB120, is seen loading in Rothesay on service 490 which runs from Port Bannatyne in the north to Kilchattan Bay in the south.**

ABOVE RIGHT: *Whiting Bay, Arran* **Arran is the largest island in the Firth of Clyde. The primary ferry service links Brodick with Ardrossan on the mainland, supplemented in the summer by one from Lochranza to Claonaig on the Kintyre peninsula. By the early 1970s bus operation had consolidated from a variety of independents down to just one, the Arran Transport & Trading Co, using the fleet name Arran Coaches. Pictured in July 1977 at Whiting Bay having just arrived from Brodick is NSJ 258M, one of several Plaxton Derwent-bodied Bedford YRQs purchased new using the government's bus grant scheme. In contrast to the situation on Bute, today the island's services are run by Stagecoach subsidiary Western Buses.**

ABOVE: *Kyleakin, Skye* **Skye is the largest island of the Inner Hebrides, connected to the mainland since 1995 by a road bridge spanning Loch Alsh. Year-round ferry services link Armadale with Mallaig, and Uig in the north of Skye with the Outer Hebrides. Pictured in September 1979 is Highland Omnibuses CD40 (PGD 216F), a Plaxton Embassy-bodied Bedford SB5 acquired with the bus operations of MacBraynes. It is about to board the ferry at Kyleakin for the short crossing to Kyle of Lochalsh on the lengthy daily service from the island's capital Portree to Edinburgh.**

LEFT: *Craignure, Mull* **The island of Mull is the second largest of those that comprise the Inner Hebrides. It is reached by three ferry routes, the main and longest one linking Craignure with Oban. Seen in August 2006 at Craignure is Van Hool Alizee-bodied DAF MB230 J782 KHD of Bowman's Coaches which had just worked service 495 from Tobermory, the island's capital town noted for its multicoloured waterfront buildings. The fleet name also references the small but popular island of Iona that lies one mile off the south west tip of Mull. In 2013 West Coast Motors acquired Bowman's and today provides all bus services.**

TOP TO BOTTOM: **Dunvegan, Skye** *Today the network of services on Skye is run by Stagecoach subsidiary Highland Country Buses. Seen in July 2015 turning into the car park at Dunvegan Castle is 27589 (SN56 AXT), an Alexander Dennis Enviro300 working service 56 from Lonmore to Portree.*

Kirkwall, Mainland, Orkney *Orkney is a collection of islands ten miles off the north coast of Scotland, which together with Shetland comprise the Northern Isles. The largest and most populated island is Mainland, where the capital town of Kirkwall and ferry port of Stromness are situated. In 1999 the Inverness-based Rapson group acquired Shalder Coaches and Peace's Coaches, giving it a virtual monopoly of bus services across Orkney. Pictured in June 2003 loading in Kirkwall on service 1B to Stromness is Optare MetroRider 46 (YSU 882), sporting the group's attractive livery and local fleet name. In 2008 operations on Orkney were taken over by Stagecoach.*

Lerwick, Mainland, Shetland *Lying over 100 miles north east of John O'Groats, Shetland is a collection of islands the largest of which, like Orkney, is called Mainland. The capital town and centre of population is Lerwick, connected by a ferry service to Aberdeen that on some days calls at Kirkwall on route. The main provider of bus services is John Leask & Son, illustrated by T40 JLS, an Ikarus Citibus-bodied DAF SB220. It is loading in Lerwick bus station on service 6 to Sandwick and Sumburgh Airport in June 2003.*

Holy Island, Northumberland *Famous as the location of Lindisfarne Castle and the ruins of a Benedictine Priory, Holy Island is accessible from the Northumberland coast by a causeway at low tide. A bus service operated by Borders Buses connects the island with Berwick-upon-Tweed on Wednesdays and Saturdays throughout the year, and on other weekdays during the summer season. On the island a frequent shuttle service links the main car park with the village and the castle. In June 2009 this was being run by island operator Douglas using P525 UGA, a Plaxton Beaver-bodied Mercedes-Benz 709D.*

LEFT: *Sheerness, Isle of Sheppey* *The Isle of Sheppey is separated from the north coast of Kent by the Swale, connected by road and rail bridges. Sheerness is the island's hub, being home to a Royal Naval dockyard that since closure in 1960 has developed into a commercial port. Historically Maidstone & District operated most bus services and today these are in the hands of Arriva. Pictured in June 2001 about to work Sheerness local service 361 is Arriva Medway Towns 5757 (E157 OMD), an Optare-bodied Leyland Olympian new to the erstwhile municipal fleet of Boro'line Maidstone.*

ABOVE: *St Helier, Jersey* *Jersey is the largest of the Channel Islands, which lie a few miles off the Normandy coast of France. The capital town of St Helier is the island's transport hub for buses and for ferry connections to Guernsey, Poole, Portsmouth and St Malo. For many years bus services were provided by Jersey Motor Transport and pictured laying over in St Helier in March 1989 is 4 (J 20513), a Willowbrook-bodied Ford R1014, one of few in the fleet not sporting an overall advertisement. Nowadays bus services are run under contract to the States of Jersey by CT Plus, part of the HCT social enterprise group, trading as LibertyBus.*

Seaview, Isle of Wight *Lying in the English Channel and separated from Hampshire by the Solent, the Isle of Wight has excellent ferry links to Southampton, Portsmouth and Lymington, plus the last remaining year-round passenger hovercraft service in the world, from Ryde to Southsea. For many years independent Seaview Services ran a bus service to Ryde, and in the mid-1980s this was rebranded as RedLynx. Seen passing through Seaview on service 12 from Nettlestone to Ryde in June 1988 is TDL 565K, an ECW-bodied Bristol RELL6G new to the island's main operator, Southern Vectis.*

BELOW: *St Peter Port, Guernsey Guernsey is the westernmost of the Channel Islands, like Jersey having its own airport, and enjoying similar ferry connections from its bustling capital, St Peter Port. In 1981 Guernseybus was formed to take over operation of the island's bus services following the collapse of the previous company. Inherited with the rolling stock was 80 (9436), a Reading-bodied Albion Nimbus, seen in St Peter Port in July 1982 still in the old Guernsey Motors livery of red and cream. The letter 'A' above the offside headlamp indicates the vehicle's width and length are suitable for traversing unrestricted on the island's narrow winding lanes.*

ABOVE: *East Cowes, Isle of Wight Whilst Ryde has the largest population on the Isle of Wight, the county town and main shopping centre is Newport. This is also the headquarters of Southern Vectis, today part of the Go-Ahead group, and Newport bus station is the hub for services that radiate across the island. Pictured promoting the island's buses in October 2009 is Southern Vectis 1111 (HW58 ASX), a Scania OmniCity leaving East Cowes on service 5 to Newport.*

BELOW: *Grandes Rocques, Guernsey In 2003 a major investment in the island's public transport saw the States of Guernsey purchase 33 narrow width East Lancs Mylennium-bodied Dennis Dart SLFs. These wore a new green and yellow livery and were leased to Island Coachways, as illustrated by 14 (70014) in July 2011 at Grandes Rocques working island circular service 7.*

LEFT: *Southwell, Portland Part of the World Heritage Jurassic Coast, Portland in Dorset is a tied island, joined to the mainland by Chesil Beach nine miles away at Abbotsbury, and connected to Weymouth by a road bridge that spans Fleet Lagoon. In 1983 Smiths of Portland restarted regular bus operation between the island and Weymouth and seen in April 1993 at the Southwell terminus is LHT 173L, an ECW-bodied Bristol RELL6G new to Bristol Omnibus but acquired from Western National, whose livery it retained. Today services on Portland are provided by First.*

All photographs by the author.

Looking back

Tim Carter turns the clock back thirty years to look at buses in Northamptonshire and Bedfordshire.

A s elsewhere in the United Kingdom, the years 1988 and 1989 were interesting times for bus enthusiasts in Bedfordshire and Northamptonshire. The biggest bus company locally was United Counties which operated 253 vehicles and had retained most of the services within the two counties when the National Bus Company operation was split on 1 January 1986. Services in the southern part of Bedfordshire went to the new Luton & District company, which ran 187 buses and served parts of Hertfordshire. Buckinghamshire-based services in and around Milton Keynes passed to another new company, Milton Keynes City Bus, with 64 buses.

In Northamptonshire some of the services in and around the county town were provided by Northampton Transport, owned by the local authority.

United Counties

United Counties had introduced minibuses to its fleet before local bus deregulation in 1986,

ABOVE: *In the summer of 1988 five new Plaxton-bodied Volvo B10Ms joined the United Counties fleet. They were in corporate Stagecoach colours and carried Coachlinks fleet names. Two are seen in Kettering bus station, with 134 (E134 ORP) in the lead.*

BELOW: *Under Stagecoach ownership United Counties in 1988 introduced Routemasters to Bedford and, as seen here, Corby, where 711 (WLT 980) is on a local service.*

including some Ford Transits in Luton. During 1986-87 United Counties standardised on Robin Hood-bodied Ivecos for minibus services, with Street Shuttle branding.

Late in 1987 the news came that Stagecoach Holdings had bought United Counties as part of the NBC privatisation process, and many enthusiasts wondered what effect that would have on services in the two counties. They didn't have long to wait, as on 1 February 1988 a fleet of eight ex-London

ABOVE: Three new Alexander-bodied Mercedes-Benz 709D minibuses were delivered to United Counties in 1989, one of which, 10 (E510 PVV), is seen in Bedford. Their stay was short and in the interests of standardisation they were soon moved to Hampshire Bus in exchange for three almost-new Ivecos.

BELOW: Long-wheelbase Leyland Olympians with Alexander bodies were added to the United Counties fleet in the summer of 1988 to replace elderly Bristol VRTs. Dundee-registered 631 (F631 MSL) was based at the company's Biggleswade garage and is seen in Bedford.

ABOVE: *A distinctive school bus livery was applied to ten Bristol VRTs in the Luton & District fleet in 1988; this example, 798 (JRP 798L), was 15 years old. The reversed lettering under the windscreen warns: Caution, school bus.*

Routemasters started operating in Bedford, followed in April by a further batch for use in Corby. Although Stagecoach had already introduced its white-based striped livery, the Routemasters were painted in United Counties green with orange, yellow and cream stripes.

To update the double-decker fleet, five Bristol VRTs were transferred from Hampshire Bus, another former NBC subsidiary now owned by Stagecoach. There were more minibuses, too, with new Robin Hood-bodied Ivecos and some second-hand vehicles. The coach fleet was updated with six Volvo B10Ms with Plaxton Paramount III 3200 bodies.

ABOVE: *Northampton Transport was one of a small number of municipal fleets to operate Bristol VRTs. Most had Alexander bodies, but six delivered in 1982 were bodied by East Lancs. This is a 1988 view of 75 (ABD 75X).*

ABOVE: *The first of Northampton Transport's Volvo Citybuses, 83 (F83 XBD), is seen in the town centre. It has an 82-seat Alexander body and was named Northampton Charter – 1189. The site on the left of the picture is now occupied by the bus station which opened in 2014.*

Deliveries in the summer of 1988 saw the arrival of Alexander-bodied vehicles, reflecting the preferred choice of the company's new owner. First were three Mercedes 709Ds, suggesting a change of type for United Counties, but they were soon swapped for three Hampshire Bus Ivecos. These were followed by 15 Leyland Olympians which were registered in Dundee; later examples would revert to the previous United Counties practice of using the Northampton licensing office. Some of those delivered in 1989 had coach seats for use on Coachlink-branded express services.

ABOVE: *Cambridge-based Cambus operated services in to Bedfordshire. This is Luton Airport with ageing Bristol RELH 156 (GCL 347N) on the X1 service from Peterborough to Heathrow Airport. The bus had been new to Eastern Counties in 1974. Its livery was an unusual pale blue.*

ABOVE: *York Bros, based in Cogenhoe, near Northampton, ran a smart fleet of coaches. New deliveries in 1988 included E70 LVV, a Volvo B10M with Plaxton Paramount III 3500 body. It is in Bedford bus station.*

Other double-deck additions to the fleet, in the winter of 1988-89, were a large batch of ex-Devon General Bristol VRTs, dating from 1980-81. These allowed the removal from service of elderly native vehicles.

Luton & District

Luton & District, which had been bought from NBC by its management in the summer of 1987, followed a similar vehicle replacement policy to that of United Counties. Iveco minibuses were selected for delivery in 1988, but with Dormobile Routemaker bodywork, rather than United Counties' choice of Robin Hood. Five Leyland Tigers with Plaxton Paramount III 3200 bodies arrived in the summer, mainly for use on the 757 Luton to London service.

Luton & District's livery was red and cream, but there were other colours in use. Some Leyland

ABOVE: *SHE 722S was the prototype Dennis Dominator which acted as a demonstrator before entering service with the South Yorkshire PTE. Like many early Dominators it had an East Lancs body. Here it is in Bedford with Cedar Coaches, operating on the service to St Neots.*

Nationals appeared in Ryanair livery when the new low-cost airline took over the sponsorship of the Luton Station to Luton Airport link. And ten Bristol VRTs were repainted as school buses. Their livery, designed to increase the awareness of other drivers, used yellow, blue, red and white, incorporating three large pencils along the sides.

Late 1988 and early 1989 saw the delivery of 12 double-deckers, these being Alexander-bodied Leyland Olympians. Two more followed in the summer, along with five Leyland Lynxes which were based at the company's depot in Hitchin, Hertfordshire. More Olympians were ordered for the autumn of 1989 by which time signs of United Counties green had all but disappeared from the Luton & District fleet.

Northampton Transport

Northampton Transport had been a council-run operation until 1986 when, to comply with government legislation, it became an arm's-length limited company, still owned by the council. This operator was not as quick as United Counties and Luton & District to start fleet replacement or introduce minibuses, but it had taken delivery of six East Lancs-bodied Leyland Olympians a couple of years before deregulation.

During 1988 eight Alexander-bodied Renault S56 minibuses joined the fleet. Four full-size vehicles were also ordered, three Alexander-bodied Volvo Citybuses and a single-deck Volvo B10M with a Duple 300 body. This had coach seats and was for use on a Northamptonshire County Council contracted service linking Northampton with Guilsborough, a village some ten miles to the north of the town.

The Citybus double-deckers were in red and cream fleet livery but with signwriting to mark 800 years of the town's charter, awarded by King Richard I in 1189, and they were soon followed by three more.

Other operators

When Milton Keynes City Bus was established it retained some of the former United Counties services linking the new city with Bedfordshire, including to Bedford where its Mercedes minibuses were regular visitors.

To the east Cambus, another former NBC subsidiary, operated into both Bedfordshire and Northamptonshire, including a service from Peterborough via Luton Airport to Heathrow Airport, and another from Peterborough to Kettering.

Independents provided a range of services in both counties including local bus routes, school and works contracts and private hire. Some of the best known among the many independents in the area were Cedar Coaches, Barfordian, Emmenton, Seamarks, Buffalo Travel and York Bros. Mullover Travel operated a park-and-ride service for Bedford Borough Council.

ABOVE: *An unusual vehicle in the Mullover fleet was this 22-seat Caetano Vianna, D207 VVV, based on an Iveco 79.14 chassis modified to allow an entrance ahead of the front axle. This coach was new to Mullover in 1986 and is providing a high standard of comfort for park-and-ride customers in Bedford.*

The hidden gem

Tucked away in a back street in the post-industrial east end of Glasgow is a bus museum. **Steve Booth**, chairman of the Glasgow Vintage Vehicle Trust, talks to Stewart J Brown.

Glasgow and its attractions have often been underrated. No matter how few people have read it in modern times, the 1930s novel *No Mean City* set the tone of Glasgow as a place of violence. The *Taggart* television crime series built on that narrative even if the leafy villages in *Midsomer Murders* are infinitely more dangerous.

But over the last three decades the city has changed dramatically, and it now draws visitors from around the world who appreciate its arts, architecture and culture. And it has not one, but two transport museums. One is the flagship Riverside Museum on the north bank of the Clyde, opened in 2011 at a cost more than £70million. The other is a hidden gem, the Glasgow Vintage Vehicle Trust's more modest Bridgeton Bus Garage, located in the city's east end, an area of fluctuating fortunes in the five decades since the garage was built in what was then a densely-populated industrial area.

TOP: *On open days shuttle services connect Bridgeton Bus Museum with Glasgow city centre. These three buses were new to Glasgow Corporation Transport. A well-loaded Daimler CVD650-30 eases past two Leyland Titans, a rear-entrance PD2 on the left and a forward-entrance PD3 on the right. The simplified livery on the PD3 was introduced in 1959.* SJB
ABOVE: *GVVT chairman Steve Booth at the wheel of his preserved ex-Greater Glasgow PTE Ailsa.* Phil Halewood

The site of the garage in Fordneuk Street was identified by Glasgow Corporation Transport in 1960, in the final phase of its bus-for-tram replacement programme. However, progress was slow, and it didn't open until 1965 when it relieved pressure on the overcrowded garage at nearby Parkhead. It was the last new bus garage built by the Corporation with an allocation of around 70 vehicles. And it had a short operational life. The city's population was declining as its industries closed. The bus fleet was being reduced. Consequently, after just 11 years Bridgeton garage was closed in 1976 by the Greater Glasgow PTE which had taken over the Corporation's bus operations in 1973. It became a transport depot for Strathclyde Regional Council and then Glasgow City Council, before once again housing buses.

The Glasgow Vintage Vehicle Trust leased the property from Glasgow City Council in 2003 and it now houses just over 120 vehicles in various states of restoration. The Trust owns a small number of these and acts as custodian for a few former Corporation buses owned by the city council, but most of the vehicles are owned by the trust's members who rent space in the garage.

Steve Booth is the trust's chairman - and owner of a nicely-preserved PTE Ailsa - and he's a man with a vision. For most visitors to a museum - any museum - it's an opportunity to look backwards. Steve and his fellow trustees are as happy to

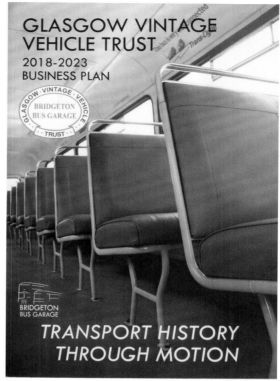

ABOVE: *A comprehensive business plan maps out the future of the GVVT.*

BELOW: *A former Glasgow Corporation AEC Regent V with Alexander body glistens in the sun outside the Riverside Museum during the 2018 West End Festival. SJB*

wallow in nostalgia as the next person, but while preserving the transport heritage of west central Scotland they must be looking forward. "It's important for the trust to be keeping the future secure," he says. Central to this is the building and the trust is in negotiations to purchase it. "We need to keep a roof over our heads," he adds. "Part of the value is keeping everything together." That includes not just the buses, central as they are to GVVT's success, but a growing archive which is housed in a hall which was originally the garage's gym, a reminder that for a business to be concerned about its employees' welfare isn't a new idea.

A comprehensive 40-page five-year business plan was published in 2018 and outlines the trust's aims and its strategies for achieving them. It's an impressive document - you can judge for yourself by reading it on the GVVT website - and reflects the professional approach the trust takes to its responsibilities.

Then there's the importance of the bus garage as an asset to be enjoyed by the local community. Steve explains: "Five years ago we ran a handful of events focussed around transport enthusiasts, who are clearly important to us. Then four years

ago we started opening one Sunday each month in the summer, aiming to attract more families."

That has proved a success and has continued. "Everybody likes a bit of nostalgia," he adds. "The vehicles are evocative. People remember the colours of the buses that used to run in the city."

And he's encouraged by the reaction of children. "Kids are amazing. They wonder why people had to get on at the back of an old bus. They ask why the driver sat in a box at the front, separated from the passengers."

The last half-cab buses entered service 50 years ago. Few remained in service 30 years ago, except in London. So, you don't have to be a child to be unfamiliar with the concept of a bus driver sitting in his "box" in splendid isolation.

To encourage family visits on the open Sundays there is a treasure hunt for children who must find Lego figures placed on buses. "We need the fun element. We can't be staid," says Steve. He hopes that if children enjoy their visit some might develop an interest in transport.

On open days and enthusiast-themed events the trust runs a shuttle service between the garage and the city centre or to the Riverside museum giving visitors a rare opportunity to ride on old

BELOW: *Services which support the West End Festival are popular with visitors. This attractive Leyland Tiger Cub is typical of coaches delivered to Alexander's in the late 1950s.* SJB

A colourful selection of mainly Scottish vehicles is housed at Bridgeton. SJB

buses. The buses attract attention from passers-by - Steve sees that when driving his own bus - and this helps raise the profile of Bridgeton Bus Garage. "The vehicles are the best publicity we have," he notes.

Buses owned or cared for by the trust and its members often take part in city events such as the annual West End Festival where a colourful selection of vehicles provides a regular service through the area. And there are one-off events like the service operated in 2018 to celebrate the 150th anniversary of the birth of the city's most famous architect, Charles Rennie Mackintosh. The buses used that day were fitted with large Mackintosh moustaches. When the weather permits open-top buses are used on services run by the trust. These are a former Glasgow Corporation 1959 Titan and an ex-Metroline 1996 Volvo Olympian which was kindly donated to the trust by West Coast Motors in 2016 after it was retired from the Glasgow City Sightseeing tour.

The first phase of a Low Emission Zone in Glasgow came in to force at the end of 2018 and will be progressively strengthened. The trust participated in the LEZ consultation and at this point does not expect it to have any impact on the services it runs. But as the rules are tightened it will be working to try to achieve an exemption for its historic buses.

Most of the buses at Bridgeton have Scottish connections and, more particularly, west of Scottish connections. There are a ten Glasgow Atlanteans, the bus that was the mainstay of the city's transport services for the best part of two decades. They are built to a variety of specifications and preserved in different liveries, a reminder that both the chassis and the Alexander body evolved during 23 years of production. There are typical Scottish Bus Group vehicles, such as Leyland Leopards with Alexander Y-type bodies, lowbridge Leyland Titans, Bristol Lodekkas, MCW Metrobuses and Leyland Olympians. There are Routemasters, a must for any self-respecting bus museum and certainly appropriate for Glasgow where they were a familiar sight on the city's streets in the late 1980s. One is in London red, the other in Kelvin Scottish blue and yellow.

Most of the buses and coaches are in the colours of well-known operators, and these include some of the smaller fleets such as A1 Service, Clyde Coast, Hutchison of Overtown, Skyeways Travel

ABOVE: *Typical Scottish Bus Group vehicles are well represented. Here are Central SMT Lodekkas and an Ailsa, followed by Western SMT Leyland Titans and a Western Lodekka.* SJB

and West Coast. At enthusiast events even more colour is added by visiting vehicles.

Not all the vehicles are on display, but Steve Booth is justifiably pleased with the way that those which are on view are exhibited in a saw-tooth display in the main area of the garage, with space to walk around them. "We don't want to cram in too many vehicles," he explains. Indeed, most vehicle owners have, as Steve puts it, "the luxury of having a drive-out space" with no need to get other buses moved to get their own bus out.

Excluding three rebodied pre-war buses, the oldest vehicle in original condition is a 1949 Maudslay Marathon III which was new to David MacBrayne, the Glasgow-based shipping, haulage and bus company which until the start of the 1970s served the western highlands and

many of the islands. The newest bus is a 2001 Dennis Trident which was generously donated by Stagecoach after a spell of duty at the Commonwealth Games in Glasgow in 2014, when Bridgeton garage was used to house some of the buses which were used to support the event. It's in Stagecoach Selkent all-over red and allows the trust to provide a wheelchair accessible bus on its open day shuttle services. The Scottish connections of a London bus? Stagecoach is based in Perth and the Trident has an Alexander ALX400 body built in Falkirk, 25 miles north-east of Glasgow.

The collection is continually evolving. "If we are to have a future we need to have a representative selection of vehicles relevant to visitors of all ages," says Steve. In this context he offers what he describes as "a worry bead": the ageing demographic of GVVT's 500-plus members. "We currently have a cross-section of members and ages with different skills who are restoring vehicles to very high standards. But how do you get younger people interested in older types of vehicles, such as Albions?" he asks.

As an organisation which depends on the skills of volunteers Steve pays tribute to their work, whether behind the scenes or up-front interacting with visitors on open days or with passengers on the shuttle services. He notes that the trust gets positive feedback on the friendliness of its volunteers. And he believes many volunteers not only enjoy whatever they originally volunteered for, but find their skills being expanded as they get drawn into other aspects of the Bridgeton bus community.

The original garage workshop area with ten pits is once again being used to service and repair buses, often handling much bigger jobs than the engineering staff would have tackled 50 years ago, when major jobs were handled at the corporation's Larkfield bus works. Today's work includes significant rectification of the bodywork on ageing buses. A separate area of the building has space for a further 12 vehicles undergoing long-term restoration.

The trust is always on the lookout for promotional opportunities. In 2018 it organised a weekend to mark the 60th anniversary of the first Leyland Atlantean entering service in Glasgow, supported by a book illustrating the history of the type in the city. That was followed in 2019 by a day celebrating 125 years since the start of municipal transport, again supported by a book. For events such as these small displays are arranged in the garage using material from the archive.

And on the subject of publishing, GVVT members receive a high-quality well-illustrated quarterly magazine, *Fare Stage*. This includes reports on current activities involving Bridgeton-based buses as well as articles looking back at buses in the west of Scotland as they once were.

The garage has an open weekend every October, geared not just to the local community but to the wider audience of bus enthusiasts and preservationists, attracting visitors and vehicles from around the UK. An intensive bus

ABOVE: *There are only five half-cab single-deckers at Bridgeton. This Duple-bodied Albion Valiant was new to Hutchison of Overtown in 1950 and has been in preservation since 1967 when it was purchased by the Albion Vehicle Preservation Trust. It is in Western SMT livery. SJB*

ABOVE: *This Atlantean was delivered to the newly-formed Greater Glasgow PTE in 1973 and has been preserved in the PTE's original livery.* SJB

BELOW: *Visiting vehicles add even more colour to an already colourful collection. This Tyne & Wear PTE long-wheelbase Leyland Atlantean AN68 attended the 2018 commemoration of 60 years since Glasgow's first Atlantean entered service.* SJB

service connects Bridgeton with the city centre and Riverside museum, run to a published timetable and with a level of organisation and efficiency that belies the fact that all involved are volunteers. Part of the garage space is cleared for traders selling transport-related artefacts without disturbing the main vehicle display.

Buses are obviously at the heart of the trust's activities. But in keeping with its aim to be an asset to the local community it is involved in other projects. Initially it worked on Scotland Against Drugs, a programme funded by the Scottish government to help recovered drug addicts get back to work. When the government funding stopped in 2006 the trust stepped in with a similar programme, Back on the Road, which involves volunteers referred by the courts, drug teams and mental health charities. This teaches not only skills which are used to help with vehicle restoration, but also what Steve describes as "soft skills" helping people who may have had challenging lives fit more comfortably in to the society around them. "We decided to take it on to help the local community," Steve explains. The challenge now is securing funding in an arena where many organisations are competing for limited financial resources.

An evocative glimpse into that aspect of Bridgeton's activities was captured in 2017 in an eight-minute documentary by film-maker Callum Rice, *Listen to Bridgeton*. It's worth watching on the BFI website if only to hear an Atlantean engine being coaxed in to life.

Steve reflects on the synchronicity of the project. "There's a parallel between rebuilding buses and rebuilding people's lives."

The main part of the building retains the air of a real bus garage which just happens to be a museum. The areas open to the public are, of course, clean and orderly ... but not what you'd call *pristine*. As a visitor you get the sense that when you're not there, people actually work in the garage and that the buses might sneak out on service. And for those visitors who are not enthusiasts, that in itself is a new experience.
www.gvvt.org

GVVT members receive an attractive quarterly magazine.

Coachwork by Strachans

Geoff Burrows (1931-2018), well known to readers of *Classic Bus* for his popular Ask Geoff column, prepared this brief history of a long-lived coachbuilder.

In 1907 James Marshall Strachan, who had been born in the north east of Scotland in 1865, joined two existing west London coach builders to form the partnership of Brown, Hughes and Strachan, building a wide range of bodywork including early double-deck motorbuses. The business worked from premises in Shepherds Bush, Park Royal and Kensington.

During the Great War the company built specialised bodies such as ambulances and field kitchens for use by the army. In 1915 the business was reconstituted as Strachan and Brown, operating from the Kensington factory of the previous partnership. The end of the war in 1918 spelt disaster for many companies that had been involved in war work, but at Strachan and Brown civilian bodybuilding was rapidly resumed, helping to replace the large numbers of buses which had been sent to the western front and destroyed.

With great confidence in the future, a site was bought in Wales Farm Road, Acton, where the company built a new factory, largely using its own labour force. This was gradually brought into use, and the building was completed in 1921. By 1922, all work had been transferred to the new factory, the last facility to move being the sawmill, after which the Kensington works was vacated.

AEC had added the company to its list of approved bodybuilders, and Strachan and Brown-bodied AECs could be found not just in Britain, but all over the world. The company built not only buses and coaches, but anything which ran on wheels, a

LEFT: *In 1950 the Ministry of Transport amended the PSV Construction & Use regulations to allow two-axle single-deck buses to be 30ft long instead of the previous 27ft maximum. On the day that the amended regulations came in to force, five Leyland Comets built to the newly-permitted length were delivered to Homeland Tours of Croydon. With 37-seat bodies these were the only 30ft-long normal-control Leylands to enter service in the UK. This photograph was taken by flash outside the Acton works at one minute past midnight to celebrate the event.*

RIGHT: *Strachans invested in a lot of expensive full-colour advertising in the transport press in the late 1940s and early 1950s.This advert appeared in* Passenger Transport *in 1950 and featured a lowbridge body on an AEC Regent III supplied to Tilstone of Burslem, Stoke-on-Trent, in 1949. The Tilstone business was taken over by PMT in 1951.*

BELOW: *This flamboyant lowbridge body for Highland Transport of Inverness was an exhibit at the 1950 Commercial Motor Show and entered service with Highland in May 1951. 72 (EST 392) was based on a Guy Arab III chassis. In February 1952 it became Highland Omnibuses E72 and was not withdrawn until 1970. It then went to work for Peace of Kirkwall. Note the company stamp on the lower right corner.*

All photographs from the author's colleciton

tradition which it maintained right through to the end of its existence. For example, at one end of the range were sports car bodies, and at the other horse boxes. The company also secured export orders, including in 1927 the bodies for some of the first trolleybuses to operate in Denmark.

The fortunes of the company took a sharp downturn in October 1928 with the departure of W E Brown. There is a story, apocryphal, that when he was asked where he was going, he replied: "Duple." His questioner retorted: "They will never amount to anything with a name like that!"

What really shook the company to the core, though, was the death of J M Strachan in 1929. The family rallied round and formed, for the first time, a limited company, Strachans (Acton) Ltd, with E Marshall Strachan as chairman and J Reith Strachan as managing director. These developments could not have come at a worse time, since the world had moved into severe depression. Sales never recovered to their former level, and the company struggled to make a living for many years.

LEFT: *In 1949 Hearn of London took five AEC Regal III coaches with 32 seats, full-width fronts and glazed cove panels. The Hearn business was bought by Tilling in 1950 and the five AECs were fitted with new ECW coach bodies in 1957, suggesting that the Strachans bodies were not of the highest quality.*

BELOW: *At first glance the Strachans bodies fitted to six AEC Swift chassis for Southampton Corporation in 1967-68 appeared to be similar to those built for London Transport. They shared the same basic structure but differed in detail. The Southampton buses were 47-seaters with AH505 8.2-litre engines. Southampton bought four more Swifts in 1969 but instead of once again supporting local industry placed the body order with East Lancs.*

One person who retained complete faith in the company all her life was the widow of J M Strachan. She acquired all the remaining shares in the company in addition to her own. In 1934 the company was again restructured under the name Strachans (Successors) Ltd. In 1961 the company was sold to the Giltspur Group with the stipulation that the Strachans name be retained for at least ten years. The Giltspur Group was itself part of a large financial organisation, with activities as diverse as night clubs and industrial packaging.

Giltspur owned a former aircraft repair factory at Hamble, in south Hampshire. It had been used, among other things, for the repair of Spitfires during the second world war. Giltspur relocated the Strachans factory and key personnel to Hamble from the Acton works which was closed and sold. The company was then renamed for the last time, as Strachans (Coachbuilders) Ltd.

For a time, the company prospered under Giltspur, and around 1970 a new factory was set up at Eastleigh to provide facilities to build the projected new Ford A-series vans. Despite considerable investment by both Ford and Giltspur, the model was doomed to failure. Changing circumstances led the Giltspur Group to close or

curtail many of its activities, and Strachans did not survive to see the end of 1974.

To describe all the products or list all the customers would require an exceptionally large volume indeed. The company built buses for the London General Omnibus Co until 1931, then concentrated on commercial vehicle contracts, many of them large, with few orders for buses although a few coaches could always be found going through the factory. The second world war gave the company plenty of variety in the types of work undertaken, and Strachans was one of the

ABOVE: *What proved to be the only Strachans double-deck trolleybus bodies were built in 1939 on AEC chassis for Southend-on-Sea Corporation. The general manager was Harold Muscroft, who had previously been at South Shields. Muscroft introduced the light blue livery to Southend on these buses, in place of the previous green. He also specified a body design which was very closely related to the Weymann trolleybuses supplied to South Shields. The six buses, 124-129 (BHJ 194-199), were withdrawn on the closure of the Southend trolleybus system in 1954.* BELOW: *Strachans' last bus model was the SC, which found use as a school bus with a number of local authorities. The most significant PSV customer was Bournemouth Corporation which took two chunky 27-seaters on Bedford VAS chassis in 1973, primarily for a town centre service. The angular lines of the SC contrast with those of the 1960s Pacerider on the following page.*

ABOVE: *The A1 cooperative, with its headquarters in Ardrossan, was an amalgam of small operators all trading under the A1 banner. In 1963 A1 members bought four 63-seat Strachans double-deck bodies, three on AEC Regent V chassis and one on a Leyland Titan PD2A/30. They were the first double-deck bodies to be built at Hamble.*

TOP RIGHT: *At the start of the 1960s a small number of operators were encouraging manufacturers to add a touch of style to the box-like bodies they were building on rear-engined chassis. Notable among those was Liverpool Corporation, whose Atlanteans had Metro-Cammell bodies with a distinctive peak on the front dome. The only half-cab double-deck body to have this feature was built by Strachans on Guy Arab V demonstrator which was registered 888 DUK.*

ABOVE RIGHT: *Ten bodies of a unique style were supplied to North Western in 1964, with an arched roof profile to allow the buses to pass under a low bridge beneath the Bridgewater Canal at Dunham Massey. North Western chose the Bedford VAL because it was the lowest suitable chassis available. The buses were 9ft 6in high. The Bedfords were 52-seaters and replaced Bristol Ls.*

RIGHT: *The 25ft-long Pacerider body was offered as a 29-seater on Bedford VAS chassis and found use both with coach operators and as welfare buses. YMB 437F was bought by Cheshire Constabulary in 1967. Attractive as the Pacerider was, Strachans couldn't compete with the coach market leaders, Duple and Plaxton.*

manufacturers chosen by the Ministry of Supply to build utility bus bodies on Guy Arab chassis. The clear majority of these were lowbridge, to an uncompromisingly square design.

An initial post-war attempt to build all-metal double-deckers was a disaster, though the company's composite bodies were usually satisfactory. Unfortunately, they were often let down by substandard quality, though there were many exceptions to this comment. Strachans also built up an extremely good relationship with the Ministry of Defence, building many hundreds of buses on Bedford SB and other chassis. These were to a rugged all-metal design which was later adapted for civilian sales.

An unusual vehicle built in the mid-1960s was the Sadler rail coach, for an entrepreneur of that name. He had hoped to interest British Railways in the concept, but despite having built one to show to BR, nothing further was heard. The vehicle languished at a disused station at Droxford., Hampshire, until it was destroyed in a fire set by vandals.

The biggest customer at the Hamble works was the Ford Motor Co. Ford's Transit van factory was only a few miles away in Southampton. Strachans had specially designed a parcel van body in cooperation with Ford to provide a high-capacity van suitable for large but light weight loads. Several thousands were built.

Naturally thoughts turned to converting one of these into a small bus. Once the idea had been proved, a contemporary design was created using the parcel van outline but with new framework underneath the skin, unlike later creations by other manufacturers. And so, the 'bread van' minibus was born.

Full-sized buses continued to be built at Hamble, though in steadily reducing numbers. The last large orders were for Wolverhampton Corporation, (Strachans' final double-deckers) and for Sunderland. There were lots of small orders by way of compensation, from private firms, local authorities, and even a few for export. In 1967 Giltspur ordered Strachans to end bus bodybuilding, but this instruction was never totally accepted.

For instance, many of the existing designs continued to attract orders from small operators, and the PSV-approved version of the Ford Transit 16-seater was selling well. Not only that, but in 1966-67 the company put together a tender for the full production order of bodies for AEC Merlins for London Transport, having supplied the original small batch of prototypes. If the company had been awarded this work, it might have survived longer.

In 1969 Strachans entered into an agreement with the Superior Coach Corporation of Lima, Ohio, in the USA. Superior bodies were to be built under licence using a combination of Strachans and Superior components, all to Superior designs. This replaced a similar arrangement which had been made in 1967 between Superior and Metro-Cammell-Weymann. One complete body and a batch of CKD (completely knocked down) components were sent to Singapore, but the arrangement was allowed to lapse.

Strachans then designed a body, the SC (for Strachans Coach), using similar construction principles with short bays. It was intended to be adaptable to fit any British bus or lorry chassis and could be supplied in kit form for export. It was to be the company's last new bus model; few found use as PSVs in Britain.

BELOW: *In 1951 Aldershot & District was still buying front-engined Dennis Lancet chassis when Dennis announced its underfloor-engined Dominant. A&D took one of the prototypes with a 41-seat Strachans bus body. The body was an uncomfortable mix of old and new, with a rather sad-looking droop to the windscreen. The centre entrance was located just ahead of the rear axle, and just look at the odd back-to-front styling of the moulding around the front wheel arch. As built the bus had a Dennis O6 engine and Hobbs automatic transmission which was soon replaced by a Dennis manual gearbox.*

Leaving London

There has been a long history of redundant London buses being used for further service elsewhere. **Geoff Mills** illustrates this with a selection of second-generation rear-engined double-deckers.

ABOVE: *Unhappy with its Fleetlines and suffering from delivery delays, London Transport bought 164 MCW Metropolitans in 1976-77. They were short-lived. Formerly MD71 in the LT fleet, KJD 271P was one of 14 London Metropolitans bought by Go Whippet of Fenstanton in 1982-83. It stands alongside an ex-London Titan in this 1998 view.*

LEFT: *London's first five MCW Metrobuses were delivered in the summer of 1978 and had smaller destination displays than later vehicles. Former M3 (THX 103S) was bought by Imperial of Rainham in 2002 and repainted in a livery evocative of the former Country Area of London Transport. It ran for Imperial until 2008.*

RIGHT: *Blue Triangle of Rainham bought several former London Metrobuses, including M463 (GYE 463W) which it acquired in 1999. Originally an independent company, Blue Triangle was bought by the Go-Ahead group in 2007.*

FAR RIGHT: *Alec Head of Peterborough operated this smart Metrobus, KYV 636X, between 2005 and 2007. It had been new as LT M636 in 1981 and carries branding for route 701 connecting Peterborough with Whittlesey and Turves.*

ABOVE: *This 1980 Metrobus, BYX 257V, formerly London M257, was converted to open top by Ensign Bus and is seen in City Sightseeing livery in Ensign ownership in 2001.*

ABOVE: *When it was new in 1983 London Titan T747 (OHV 747Y) carried a gold livery, sponsored by Leyland Bus, to mark 50 years since the formation of the London Passenger Transport Board. It was repainted red in 1984, but when purchased by Sullivan Buses of Potters Bar in 2000, its new owner recreated the original anniversary colours. It still carried this livery when photographed in 2012 in the ownership of Talisman Coach Lines of Great Bromley. operating a shuttle service to the Clacton Air Show.*

ABOVE: *Go Whippet bought several Titans from London including former T911 (A911 SYE) acquired in 1996 when it was 13 years old and converted to single door layout, which increased its seating capacity from 70 to 76. It is seen in Cambridge in 2002.*

LEFT: *The conversion of T1020 (A620 AHV) was not as neat as that on the Go Whippet bus, with thick pillars on either side of the window located where the exit door had been. It had several owners after being withdrawn by London Buses in 1997, including Garnetts of Bishop Auckland. The livery promotes the company's tours.*

ABOVE: *T1020 again, now in the ownership of Talisman Coach Lines in 2014, looking smart in London red, complete with roundel. It is at Parkeston Quay with the cruise ship Brilliance of the Seas as a backdrop.*
BELOW: *When it's time in London was up, Arriva London transferred what had been Metrobus M1289 (B289 WUL) to Colchester, where it operated from 1999 to 2001. This photograph was taken in Colchester High Street soon after the 14-year-old bus arrived from London.*

All photographs by the author.

Coast to Coast

South Coast dweller **David Jukes** finally realised a long-time ambition to visit West Coast Blackpool in the summer of 2018. Here's what he found.

Blackpool. The UK's favourite seaside resort and home to the Tower, Illuminations, Pleasure Beach and Zoo. And, home to Britain's only surviving first-generation tramway, which was significantly upgraded into a light rail system between 2009 and 2012. It is operated by Blackpool Transport, one of the UK's few remaining council-owned bus – and tram – operating companies.

It was a long-held wish to visit Blackpool (about 30 years or more to be honest) but one that was finally realised in August 2018 when Mrs J booked a week's break in the resort, no doubt fed up with me saying: 'Must go to Blackpool this year,' when planning holidays and bus event visits each spring.

We may have missed the pre-upgraded tramway and step-entrance bus fleet, but Blackpool did not disappoint (just as well given its distance from our

ABOVE: *Current mainstay of the Blackpool Transport fleet is the ADL Enviro400 City, of which 55 were delivered in 2016-17. 454 (SN67 WZV), new in 2017, passes St Mary's Roman Catholic Church in Lord Street, Fleetwood.*
BELOW: *Heading south along the Promenade is heritage-liveried Blackpool Transport 332 (PF06 EZP), a 2006 East Lancs Lolyne-bodied Dennis Trident.*

ABOVE: *In 2012-13 Blackpool Transport acquired 19 East Lancs Lowlander-bodied DAF DB250s from the Isle of Man. The DAFs had been new in 2001-02. Nine remained in service in August 2018 including 372 (J900 BTS) which was originally Isle of Man Transport 55 (FMN 497T).*
LEFT: *Blackpool's main industry is tourism. ADL Enviro400 City 406 (SN16 OVG) heads north past one of the Golden Mile's many amusement arcades.*
Below: *Blackpool Transport Services acquired five four-year-old Wright Eclipse Urban-bodied Volvo B7RLEs from Anglian Bus in 2010, including 523 (AU06 BPK) seen at North Pier.*

Portsmouth home!) and reminded me of childhood days spent on Southsea seafront but with the bonus of railed transport along the prom.

Blackpool Transport Services

Blackpool Council-owned Blackpool Transport Services operates the 11-mile-long Blackpool Tramway between Starr Gate and Fleetwood – with a branch from the North Pier to Blackpool North railway station under construction at the time of our visit – and bus services within Blackpool, Fylde and the surrounding area.

The primary tramway service is provided by 18 purple and white Bombardier Flexity 2 articulated trams supplied in 2011-12 (fleet numbers 001 to 016) and 2017 (017/8), known as the A-fleet. Supporting these is the B-fleet formed of nine modified former Blackpool Corporation English Electric double-deck Balloon trams of 1934/35 vintage with 700-series fleet numbers.

All the B-fleet trams were modified between 2009 and 2012 with widened centre doorways to enable use of the Supertram platforms. Four were previously reconstructed between 1998 and 2004 with flat ends as Millennium Cars. Their intended use as extras during visitor peak periods was

evidently rare with several stored out of service and operational examples showing evidence of heritage fleet usage – more of which later.

Bus services are operated by the 130-strong mainly double-deck fleet. The black and yellow Blackpool Transport livery introduced in 2010 was still in evidence on the East Lancs Lolyne-bodied Dennis Tridents delivered between 2002 and 2006, plus the remaining ex-Bus Vannin (Isle of Man) East Lancs Lowlander-bodied DAF DB250s of 2001 vintage acquired in 2012.

Single-deckers in this livery were four of the five 2006 Wright Eclipse Urban-bodied Volvo B7RLEs acquired from Anglian Bus when they were four years old. The other, plus one Trident, carried an earlier cream and green livery.

The premium Palladium brand with a grey and pale-yellow livery was introduced to the town in 2015 on a batch of Mercedes-Benz Citaros fitted with Wi-Fi, e-leather seating and more. These features, plus the branding and livery, also appear on nine refurbished 2010 Plaxton Centro-bodied Volvo B7RLEs, 55 Alexander Dennis Enviro400 Citys delivered in 2016-17 and 18 Alexander Dennis Enviro200 MMC midibuses delivered earlier in 2018.

ABOVE: *Outside Blackpool Tower is Palladium-branded Blackpool Transport 530 (BF60 UVO), a 2010 Plaxton Centro-bodied Volvo B7RLE.*

LEFT: *The Palladium brand was introduced in 2015 by Blackpool Transport on a batch of Mercedes Benz Citaros which included 551 (BJ15 GOK), seen on the Golden Mile.*

RIGHT: *Heritage tram tours meet at North Pier. Balloon 715 on the left, new in 1935, is about to terminate while Boat 600 on the right, which dates from 1934, heads south for the Pleasure Beach.*

RIGHT BELOW: *Departing from the South Pier bus stop is Catch 22 Bus Y381 GAX, a 2001 Plaxton Pointer 2-bodied Dennis Dart SLF new to Cardiff Bus as its 381 and retaining its former owner's livery upon which 21 Coastliner branding has been applied.*

BELOW: *Flexity 004 heads north through North Albert Street, Fleetwood, bound for the Ferry terminus, the northernmost end of Blackpool's tram service. The Flexity trams have 74 seats and can carry up to 148 standing passengers.*

Heritage Tram Tours

It was feared the £100million light rail upgrade funded by the government, Lancashire County Council and Blackpool Council would spell the end for the traditional Blackpool tram in its home town, save the B-fleet Balloons and the three illuminated trams remaining in Blackpool Transport ownership. The net result of lobbying Blackpool Council was the establishment in 2014 of the Blackpool Heritage Trust to promote the retention, preservation and continued operation of Blackpool's heritage tramcars. Heritage Tram

Tours is operated by Blackpool Transport Services alongside the regular Flexity-operated service but does not form part of its commercial operation, with trams crewed by volunteers and farebox revenue covering operational costs. Restoration outlays are reliant upon the generosity of others.

The principal tour operation is the two-tram Promenade Tour between the Pleasure Beach and North Pier/Tower with some journeys extended north to the Cabin. This operates every weekend from February to November and daily during school holidays. There are also several Gold Event weekends

ABOVE: *Operating Catch 22 Bus Coastliner route 21 at North Pier is Manchester Bus Tours' V158 MEV, a 1999 Alexander ALX400-bodied Dennis Trident new to Selkent as its TA158 and more recently Golden Tours 158, for which it was converted to partial open-top layout for London sightseeing.*

with tours to Bispham, Cleveleys and Fleetwood, with other special workings and pre-booked tours available. The heritage tram fleet is based at Rigby Road Depot, around which I was given a tour by James Millington, the Heritage Fleet Manager (the family for some reason decided the Pleasure Beach was their preferred destination that day) and includes examples of most Blackpool tramcar types from the 1920s Standards onwards. The majority are owned by the Blackpool Heritage Trust with others loaned to the Trust by individuals, museums and other organisations and groups. Also kept at Rigby Road are the B-fleet Balloons and Millennium Cars

plus other tramcars stored for private owners.

Not all are operational, but over our week's stay we were able to enjoy tours on Standard 147, Boat 600 plus Balloons 715 and 717 – all providing an excellent and most enjoyable way to experience Blackpool's seafront for an inexpensive £3.50 return each (£2 child) with day tickets also available.

Other Operators

Also seen regularly on Blackpool's promenade were vehicles from the Stagecoach Merseyside and South Lancashire fleet operating its Preston to Blackpool route 68. Without exception, those spotted were

ABOVE: *Loading in Fleetwood's Albert Square on 9 August is Preston Bus 20769 (PO56 RNZ), a 2006 Optare Solo M850 28-seater which was originally numbered 69 in the Preston Bus fleet before the company was acquired by Rotala in 2011.*
LEFT: *Approaching journey's end in Blackpool with its destination screen set for the return journey to Preston is Stagecoach Merseyside and South Lancashire ADL Enviro400-bodied Scania N230UD 15572 (PX59 CUW).*

ABOVE: *Coaches play a significant role in bringing visitors to Blackpool. The North Promenade is host to WSC 267 of Whitestar of Neilston, near Glasgow. It is a 2016 VDL Futura 2 which was originally registered SF16 KUU.*

PX59-registered Alexander Dennis Enviro400-bodied Scanias – identical to those operated by Stagecoach South on my route 700 Coastliner commute!

In evidence, too, were Catch 22 Bus vehicles on its Coastliner 21 service. Former Cardiff Plaxton Super Pointer Dart SLFs in their previous owner's orange livery ran alongside a Manchester Sightseeing-liveried Dennis Trident open-topper of sister company Manchester Bus Tours.

And spotted at Fleetwood in between the trams and Blackpool double-deckers was an Optare Solo of Preston Bus on its route 75, Fleetwood to Preston.

Blackpool's status as a seaside resort ensures the presence of several touring coaches from across the UK. These had to find me as I knew a tour of the town's coach parks would never form part of the holiday itinerary, although I think I got away with the heritage tram rides.

In closing I am pleased to say we made good use of Blackpool's public transport – and our feet – during our stay, with the car remaining untouched on the hotel forecourt all week. The train will take the strain next time – we aim to be back within the next few years to experience the Illuminations and the latest heritage tram restorations.

www.blackpoolheritage.com

ABOVE: *Blackpool has long been popular with Scottish holidaymakers. This 2018 tri-axle Scania K410EB6 Interlink belongs to John Hunter of Tullibody and carries personalised registration JH18 JAH. The Interlink is built in Finland.*

Grampian
in retrospect

Billy Nicol looks back at Grampian Transport, the principal
operator of local services in Aberdeen, as it was 25 years ago.

ABOVE: *The favoured double-decker of Grampian Transport in the 1970s and early 1980s was the Leyland Atlantean with
Alexander's peak-domed style of bodywork. 263 (HRS 263V) of 1980 is seen in Broad Street in 1995 with Marischal College in
the background.*

ABOVE: *GRT Holdings, Grampian's parent company, owned several other businesses, including Northampton Transport. In 1993 all six East Lancs-bodied Olympians in the Northampton fleet were transferred to Aberdeen, although their stay in the city was brief. Northampton, like Grampian, favoured two-door buses. The Olympians had been new in 1984.*

BELOW: *Like many other operators, Grampian switched to Leyland's Olympian when Atlantean production ended. Those bought new had Alexander R-type bodies, including this bus from the first batch of Olympians, delivered in 1984. Most of Grampian's Olympians had Gardner engines.*

ABOVE: *A small but varied fleet of small buses was operated by Grampian and marketed as Beaver bus - an appropriate name for this Mercedes-Benz 709D with Reeve Burgess Beaver bodywork. It was one of six delivered in 1991.*
BELOW: *Later 709Ds included nine in 1993 with Alexander (Belfast) bodywork.*

ABOVE: *Grampian operated Alexander-bodied Renaults alongside the more common Mercedes. Three S56s were transferred from Northampton Transport in 1994. They were seven years old.* ABOVE RIGHT: *Some of the Mercedes O405s had Optare Prisma bodies, built to a high specification. One is seen soon after delivery in the summer of 1995. By 1997 Grampian would be running 35 Prismas.*

ABOVE: *GRT was one of the pioneers in raising the standards of the buses it operated, for a time specifying air-conditioning and double-glazing. These are features of this 1993 Mercedes-Benz O405 with Wright Cityranger body. It was one of a batch of 14.* BELOW: *The pride of the fleet? New in late 1992 was a Mercedes-Benz O405G articulated bus with Alexander body. It was numbered 1 and registered K1 GRT. It was the first articulated bus for the UK since a batch of Leyland-DABs for South Yorkshire in 1985. It was 17.6m long, had three doors, 60 seats and could carry up to 50 standing passengers.*

ABOVE: *In 1994 Grampian Transport was running an open-top tour in Aberdeen using this 1967 Alexander-bodied Atlantean which had been new to Grampian's predecessor, Aberdeen Corporation Transport. The Corporation had a long history of running city tours, although not with open-toppers.* BELOW: *Grampian's last ten Olympians in 1988 differed from previous deliveries in being long-wheelbase models. This increased their seating capacity from 73 to 78. The longer Alexander bodies had an additional short side window.*

I could have loved you better

All photographs by the author.

Robert E Jowitt dwells with affection bestowed far too late on the thoroughly classic Parisian Somua OP5 and its close relations.

I t is sometimes the case, perhaps sadly, that a very splendid object, even a bus, must be eclipsed by another object, another bus in this matter, even more fine. In my own experience I must apply such category to the Somua – or latterly Saviem – OP5 in service in Paris as introduced in the late 1940s.

I was brought up to believe, by my father and his experiences of Paris, that the only proper Paris bus was one with an open platform at the back, as applied to a pre-1914 postcard in his possession and a pre-1939 Dinky Toy given to me

ABOVE: *In 1966, passing the eastern flank of the Gare du Nord on conduit tram-track closed some three decades earlier, an OPS5 heads towards a bus stop next a classic café.*

soon-post-1945. I was vaguely aware nevertheless, thanks to early pages of *Buses Illustrated*, that there were more modern buses too. These included the Somua OP5. From my first visit to Paris in 1960 I brought home a Dinky Toy OP5, to which my father instantly objected because it was not an open-rear platform. I remain nevertheless very fond of it to this day.

As a matter of history, throughout the earlier

1930s the Paris transport authorities had, along with vast tram scrapping, introduced a fleet of hundreds of motor buses, firstly of profile dating back with little change to 1916 but suddenly from 1936 in streamlined fashion (by the view of the time) with the Renault TN4H, still with open platform (if sadly diminished in dimensions from *la belle époque*).

A major quantity of this lovely new fleet became dispersed with, in 1940, the invasion of the enemy and the fall of France, buses sent out rescuing government archives or carrying troops or heaven knows what other purpose, probably sometimes evil, with the result that by the end of the war Paris was desperately short of buses to provide any sort of public service.

Authority picked up whatever it might find off the shelf, suitable for rural rides, nothing else being then available at that moment even for the streets of Paris, and then emerged in 1950 with a proper urban bus, namely the Somua OP5. It has been stated that the initials OP indicated *Omnibus Parisien*, a claim which I could consider open to doubt. The 5, it is guessed, may have referred to the new decade; after all, in the case of the Chausson, the suffix 52 meant it was introduced in 1953. I cannot resist, however, the argument that the vehicle was closely related in

style to its predecessor of ten years earlier, the Renault TN4H, especially the so-called *banlieue* or suburban version of same with the entrance enclosed on the side of the platform. In the OP5 modernity was added by a door ahead of the front axle – such as a TN4H never knew – and the driver now had no bulkhead between him and his passengers, but instead the luxury of a Wilson pre-selector gearbox. The side windows came with rounded rather than right-angle bottom corners, not traditional, but the frontal windscreen pattern retained something of the aura of tragic dog-eyes familiar on the TN4H, with a radiator grille not too different in shape from a sporting Bugatti.

The green and cream livery familiar for many decades remained, but in the Somua case we must heed a couple of variations. One hundred bodies were built by the RATP Central Workshops (*Atelier Central*) for city work with the cream coming down under the windows to below the route boards on the side, the last time this scheme was to be seen, while the 200 for suburban use were manufactured by MGT (*Million-Guiet-Tubauto*) and had the route boards backed by the lower green. Those from the *Atelier Central* were probably the very last wooden frames for Paris, the MGT lot being all metal. The most curious matter on these buses was that while they retained the

ABOVE: *A quartet at the Porte de Montmartre terminus, 1969. Note the prominent route number display.*

Typical Paris street scene one.

absolutely classic *capot de ligne* (route number box) – archetypal since 1916 – they adopted the strange habit of stuffing the route blind, until now by heredity just below the number and just above the protruding 'peaked cap' of the canopy, into an untoward space in the top of the nearside windscreen.

This reverted – thank Heaven or *Grace a Dieu* – to a fairly classic pattern in 1955, in other words with destination box above the lip of the canopy – but we here encounter a central door to speed passenger movements; at this moment the bus became the OP5-3, the final 3 indicating the number of doors, which rendered the OP5-3 in these later years a well-advanced conception of modern urban bus use. It should be noted that due to not unusual vicissitudes or take-overs in the French vehicular industry the name of Somua was replaced towards the end of the run by the marque of Saviem, though with little other visual effect. In total the Somua or Saviem contingent reached about 681 examples. I cannot resist, as an observer much bewitched by the magic of fleet numbers, pointing out that as part of the curious Paris habit (not in truth unique) of taking numbers from scrapped vehicles for the newest entry meant that

the OP5 included such delightful numbers as 555, 999, 1000 and 1001, which numerically speaking were well below those issued to the classic Renault and Panhard series, these being from 1638 to 4527 in the period 1931-1938.

Then to pass to number one. It is too hazardous a game here to try to ascertain its origins in the pre-1914 period, or whether it may have shown on the first Schneider H of 1916. (Someone somewhere may offer more precise details, but the only man I knew who could have done, J-B Prudhommeaux, died near half a century ago, perhaps feeling that with the last of the Paris open-platforms taken off the roads life was no longer worth living.) I do know however that number one materialised in 1947 in a small batch (18 items) of off-the-peg almost utterly rural Chausson APH47, committed to re-start service in the Parisian suburbs.

Such unsuitable vehicles enjoyed but a short life and fell to the scrapyard in face of the Berliet PCP and then PCS of 1955-1960 of which 150 were built. It must be admitted instantly that the bodywork here was to all intents and purposes identical to sister OP5-3, but round the front this bus – which some parties may care to declare as indeed indistinguishable - somehow, despite an attempt at the drooping windscreen, failed entirely to capture the classic *chien-triste* eyes of the OP5. The heavy chrome bars across the radiator, even if intended to be stylish, proved in truth coarse or un-alluring. In Lyon or Marseille, on the front of three-axle trolleybuses or buses as the case might be, such crude design was acceptable, but was ever wrong in Paris; the PCP - simply by some subtle difference in the lower curve of the windscreen - could never claim the tragic-dog look.

Sad to relate, later or final offerings of both Paris series suffered the insult of having the famous route-number box chopped off (no!, not really!- merely excluded from the design!) and replaced by a bland – and to some eyes ugly – box containing number and screen in a line together, probably sensible in new tastes but not what the traditional eye desired. Some of the vehicles, moreover, succumbed to dire experiments in windscreen development as a prelude to the shocking cylindrical design which became the hallmark of the Standards, the Saviem SC10 and the Berliet PCM-R, and other matters entirely to be eschewed in these paragraphs. It was among the Berliet PCP atrocities here, if I recall correctly, that number one once more reared its head. I saw the bus in question, when in the 1935 Renault which I had just acquired from the RATP in 1970, being

driven by a useful member of the Paris Transport Museum through the northern suburbs of Paris towards Le Havre. We followed for a few stops, it being on active service on the road my friend had chosen to drive. I suppose I ought to have tried to press for attempting a photo shot, such as might at that moment have been titled *ancien et moderne*, but I could find little merit in the bus with number one and the effort anyway would have been enormous. Perhaps hardly surprisingly I never saw number one again.

It may be gathered from the above circumstances that the Renaults were in rapid decline with the last streamlined TN4H being withdrawn in January 1971. From here on, please remark, they were to be followed a couple of years later by both OP5 and Berliet PCP. It is doubtless debatable whether we should draw comparisons on how the TN lasted 35 years while its replacement lasted ten years less. Blame it on the all-conquering Standard.

I see now, that regardless of – or even regarding! – all that I have said above, I must esteem the OP5 as a thoroughly classic bus, one which in its place and time deserved much attention, and I must be forever sorry that I did not at the time serve it as such.

Meanwhile, with the final scrapping of the Renault TNs I had acquired two (one as mentioned

ABOVE: **At Choisy in 1966 beside a typical dark, dank terminus shelter we find the final form of OP5-3 with route number alongside the destination screen instead of in a box above, a sad descent from tradition.**

ABOVE: *The face of the 1955 Somua OP5 bore considerable resemblance to that of the 1936 Renault TN4H.*
BELOW: *Typical Parisian street scene two, Boulevard St Michel. On Sundays in 1970 route 21, operated by TN4Hs on weekdays, was given over to OP5s, presumably for one-man operation and economy.*

ABOVE: *Stormy weather ... Somua 1000, a most meritorious number, clearly shows that despite having a front door the position of the driver is not that much different from memories of the TN4H.*

above), transported them to England, and I have been condemned ever since to suffer or verily to enjoy vastly the vagaries of living with them. As for the idea of an OP5... well, hmmm!

Turning for a moment from such consequence I must dwell on diverse side-lines or look-alikes branching from the original OP5

Whether or not OP stood for *Omnibus Parisien*, the only city anywhere else in France to adopt the OP5, barring one solitary example in Lyon, was Strasbourg. I will attend here first to that lonely Lyonnais. It was brought in on trial in 1950, and subsequently purchased as being of noteworthy quality. It appeared almost identical to the Paris OP5-3, except that the central door had two leaves, not four. It was numbered as 1001 in the Lyon fleet, and designated as OP8, though what might be the significance of the 8 is beyond my comprehension. It was not followed up in Lyon because it proved in the eyes of the Lyon operators decidedly too expensive.

I regret I have never done more than travel by train through Strasbourg, city of many timber-framed and art-nouveau architectural gems, but by various chances I know it operated a certain number of OP5-3, not much above 50 in all, in two batches, the first 16 entering service from late 1953 and early 1954. These differed from their Paris sisters mainly by virtue of a large and conspicuous ventilation system on the roof round the route number box and destination blind, a veritable camel's hump, though whether this protuberance was intended for the benefit of the passengers or, in the case of the trolleybuses mentioned hereinafter for cooling of electrical equipment, I remain sufficiently mechanically ignorant to furnish an answer. Livery smacked somewhat of ornithology, the body in general being a greyish blue while the sides of the radiator grille and the front bumper were scarlet, thus, with a little imagination, the shades of a bullfinch. The further 38 later deliveries retained the bullfinch colour but abandoned the camel's hump, and thus more and very closely resembled their Parisian companions. Subsequently some at least were repainted in red and cream, perhaps to match the Standards which, nevertheless, evicted them in 1966. Records suggest that the Strasbourg OP5 was equipped to haul a trailer, and with the German influence in the city (it has in history exchanged nationality at various times) the use of trailers is hardly unusual. In arguably further Teutonic style the roofs of several of the OP5-3 were decorated with side advertising boards, many of them boasting one or another of the splendid range of the local beers of Alsace. The beers of course are still available, but

ABOVE: *Be the artistic qualities of the Left Bank as they may, the Berliet PCP, even when observed in that quarter, lacked – at least in this author's eyes – the artistic merit of the OP5. Was it that the curve below the windscreen was not as pronounced as that on the OP5? Subtle, perhaps, but invidious enough to prove very unpleasant.*

naturally not the buses.

To add to the Strasbourg story, and to lead to other relevant issues, it becomes necessary to append some trolleybus tales.

Paris in the war, to keep bus traffic moving in face of petrol penury, had introduced four suburban trolleybus lines, with vehicles typical of small provincial systems, presumably the only goods on offer. These were replaced by the Vetra VBR of 1948, its bodywork having many affinities to the TN4H, and then the VBF of 1957, with bodywork closely allied to the OP5. Both were very decent vehicles withal, even though lacking the sad-dog-eye windscreen. But Paris despatched all this in 1966, though as we shall see not quite to eternity.

Out to the east Strasbourg installed a couple of trolleybus routes, in 1948-49, with again the Vetra VBR, but here plus the camel's hump ventilator round route number and destination, this preceding the similar contraption on the OP5 by five years; but all this was adding to the atmosphere or spirit of the post TN4H era.

In 1961 Strasbourg fell out of love with the trolleybus, selling five to Grenoble and three to Le Havre. Paris followed from 1963 to 1966. Hence went 38 VBF to Grenoble, where they looked quite at home in the quasi-Parisian architecture of boulevards, even if the vistas at the ends of these boasted snow-clad Alps. Limoges, in the bleak uplands of the Massif Central, appears to have taken on the balance of the Paris VBRs.

If it can be accepted that these trolleybus adventures carried forth the likeness of the Somua, it lingered, though Grenoble scrapped its VBR specimens in 1968 and Le Havre followed late in 1970, thus before OP5 death in Paris around 1972. The VBF survived with a background of white mountains in Grenoble another ten years; and in Limoges they hung on even longer. I was travelling through France in the spring of 1989, in pursuit believe it or not of Saviem Standards which in their turn were fast fading, and thus attacked Limoges, which besides Standards, was also operating modern trolleybuses, though I did not actually see the latter as they did not run on Sundays which happened to be the day of my visit.

Yet a couple of interim memories may merit

mention. If, even into the early 1980s, you took a train from the Gare d'Austerlitz towards the south west of France, you could see some few kilometres out, up on a hillside to the west, a glimpse next a thoroughly suburban little house, what looked as if it must be an original OP5. I never found out more about it. Meanwhile, when I was first in possession of my TN4H, driving to rallies and such like here and there in England, English persons (two at least, perhaps three or four?) would approach me and say, 'I saw a bus just like this in Tours on my holiday not long ago'. In due season I passed through Tours myself, and lo and behold, in a very murky rush hour amidst many up-to-date buses, saw a vision of green and cream (if grubby – probably with a contractor) plough its furrow; but it was no TN, it was a pretty original OP5. I am fairly convinced that this was the bus those British wanderers had seen, and it says much for the family likeness that they believed truly they had witnessed a 1936 Renault. Other commitments prevailing I was unable to pursue this matter further.

With less resemblance to Renault, being in scarlet and cream, but again in a bus rush hour, now in the city of Arles in the south of

ABOVE: *Except for the windscreen the ex-Paris VBF trolleybus in Grenoble in the early 1970s, albeit in red and cream, is almost exactly in OP5 character, even unto Parisian style route-boards on the side.*
BELOW: *Typical Parisian street scene three. The Somua fast ousting the very senior Renault in the background little dreams it has itself only two or three years to live …*

ABOVE: *In Grenoble surroundings which could almost pass for Paris the ex-Paris VBF trolleybus looks thoroughly at home. In truth these streets are probably more salubrious than those of the Paris suburbs as encountered in earlier experience.*

France with some if not many of the famed opera-hymned beauties straying in low and dusty sunlight along the pavements, came another glorious vision. Though deprived of its route-number box, and even in the livery just mentioned, there could be no doubt of its origin; and this was around the date when the last of them were still being cast out. Unlike the Tours case I managed in the next un-dusty daylight somehow to track it to one of its termini, where its driver proudly exhibited to me the slap-on magnetic plate for its route. Holders for Parisian style route-boards remained, now useless. The Parisian interior was pretty well intact. Back in England I wrote to its Bouches-du-Rhone operators offering to buy it, and received a somewhat curt reply, implying my request was cheeky, as they had not long purchased it themselves. I suppose, looking back on experience, that I should be grateful for this brush-off.

One more, then, herewith no question of brush-off for, though probably the same period, I never even dreamed of approaching the owners. On some journey involving a traverse of Paris, towards or into nightfall, the details now entirely escaping me, I found myself outside the Gare St Lazare. There, by the pavement, was the familiar silhouette, but now in the dark and light grey of the vehicles of the police. A livery all too familiar in the streets of Paris, not that I ever fell foul of it myself (of course!). I accosted the driver, told him I recognised what his charge had formerly been. He seemed pleased enough with my interest and told me the present purpose was *pour ramasser les vagabonds*. A splendid phrase, to gather in the tramps and vagrants. It could be felt that such was an ignoble role for a once splendid bus, but surely actually a worthy task. Where, after all, would we be without dustcarts; I have seen the streets of Paris in a dustmen's strike, I do not think I would want to see them if there was no service for the vagabonds. That bus was surely as valuable in its new guise as might have been an ex-Paris revival in Arles red-and-cream preservation. None can last for ever, any more than can their owners or drivers or fanciers…

In the end, nevertheless, I cannot resist wishing I had given the OP5 all the admiration it deserved; or, as the renowned Tom Paxton was singing at about that time *'It's a lesson too late for the learning,'* and *'I could have loved you better!'*

Down south, near Arles in 1972, this ex-Paris OP5 has lost its route-number box but not much else; and if this lack appears odd, the creature looks very smart in Lyon-style red and cream, even though the new Bouches-du-Rhone owners' paint job has not appreciated livery-wise the curve below the windscreen. At this moment, in Paris, her sisters were probably nearly all dying or even dead.

All photographs by the author.

A Bournemouth based holiday

In August 1974 **Mike Greenwood** had a holiday in the Bournemouth area.
He shares some recollections of the changing scene.

was fortunate to go on family holidays to Bournemouth in July of 1968, 1969 and 1970, but with me still being in my early teens I only managed to take 12 black-and-white photos with my Zeiss Nettar camera on the 1970 holiday. However, I enjoyed watching and riding on Bournemouth's trolleybuses in 1968 and then sadly saw lots of them parked up in the Mallard Road depot in 1969, with them having finished the previous April.

I was also enthralled by the large and varied Hants & Dorset bus and coach fleet, with its Tilling ownership contrasting in fleet colour and chassis/body combinations with that of Midland Red

in my home town of Leicester. The magnificent Royal Blue coaches also impressed me, and I was bemused by the quirky location of the Royal Blue depot in Rutland Road, Charminster. This was a throwback to Royal Blue's evolution with it being one of the premises of Elliott Brothers, the company's founders. All these aspects made a significant impression on me.

By 1974 my Aunt Doris was resident in Bournemouth having moved from Bexhill. A positive response was received when I asked whether I could stay with her for a week in the summer and the dates from August 3 to 10 were set. Accordingly, I booked a return ticket

ABOVE: *Bristol FS6B 1105 (5667 EL) waits to depart for Bournemouth from the attractive bus station at Lymington on 6 August. New in May 1960 it had a 60-seat ECW body, fitted with platform doors and a sun visor over the driver's windscreen.*

LEFT: *On the first day of my holiday, Saturday 3 August, I made my way to Swanage where I caught Hants & Dorset Bristol MW6G 1828 (7118 LJ) to Corfe Castle. This ECW-bodied coach was new to Hants & Dorset in May 1962 as a 39-seater numbered 882. Despite being demoted to one-man stage-carriage operation in September 1969 it retained 37 coach seats, albeit without the headrests. It had been renumbered 1828 in September 1971 as part of the renumbering scheme which combined the Hants & Dorset and Wilts & Dorset fleets.*

BELOW: *Also photographed in Lymington on the same date is 1688 (JKK 183E) a 1967 ex-Maidstone & District 45-seat Willowbrook bodied Leyland Panther PSUR1/1R which had been acquired in 1972. A total of 17 Panthers had been purchased from M&D between December 1971 and July 1972. 1688 is working the short route 121 to Lymington Pier. White and orange circles above the fleet number denote that it is allocated to Lymington garage.*

with Associated Motorways for the Leicester to Bournemouth coach service which involved a change at the famous Cheltenham interchange. I had enjoyed watched the 2pm departure from Cheltenham on many occasions and was, therefore, mindful of the chaotic scenes as thousands of passengers were all trying to make their connections and often getting in each other's way! I was aware that in the summer season there was also an incredibly early morning interchange time, at 2am from memory, and I thought that this would be a less intensive affair, so I booked the late evening departure from Leicester for Friday August 2.

On arrival at Cheltenham I soon discovered my assumption was completely wrong! It was just as busy but this time travellers were also extremely tired which probably made matters worse. I can't find any notes now of which coaches I rode on that Friday night/Saturday morning but I'm fairly sure it was a splendid Black & White Motorways machine on each leg. I do, however, remember waking up on the second leg of the journey just to see a dramatic dawn breaking over Salisbury Plain on a perfect summer's morning.

The plan during my holiday was to use Bournemouth as a base with visits to Corfe Castle, Lymington, Parkstone, Poole, Ringwood, Sandbanks, Southampton, Swanage and Winchester during the week.

In 1974 I had disposable income having been employed for two years in the offices at Leicester City Transport. This had enabled me to purchase

ABOVE: *From Lymington I travelled on to Southampton where I photographed 43-seat Bristol MW5G 856 (HEL 390D), which was new in August 1966, and is passing the impressive Hants and Dorset Omnibus Station building - the lettering is just visible above the roof of the bus. The MW had received a repaint into NBC poppy red livery in July 1973.*

LEFT: *Also photographed in Southampton making its way back to the garage following the evening peak is 1235 (FLJ 155D) which had also been new in 1966. It was delivered as an FLF6B but was then converted to an FLF6G in October 1972 with a Gardner 6LW engine replacing its Bristol BVW unit. It had the standard ECW 70-seat body but with the Cave-Brown-Cave heating system, identifiable by the grilles flanking the destination display.*

BELOW: *I also made my way to the Southampton garage and works in Bedford Place where I photographed 1642 (UEL 562J), a 50-seat ECW-bodied Bristol RELL6G which carried this dual-purpose livery.*

a Nikkormat FTN camera which allowed me to start perfecting my photographic skills and make the move from black-and-white into colour using a mixture of Agfa CT18, Agfachrome 50S and Kodak Kodachrome II transparency films.

The Hants & Dorset and Wilts & Dorset subsidiaries of the Tilling group had both passed to the National Bus Company (NBC) on January 1, 1969. The operators then merged in 1972 under the Hants & Dorset name and management. However, rather than Hants & Dorset's green, the enlarged operation adopted the fleet livery of National poppy red. The new operation covered routes from Pewsey in the north, Poole to Fareham in the south, Basingstoke in the east, and Shaftesbury and Warminster in the west.

At the time of my visit there was a great deal going on. The fleet was still in the process of being repainted so there was an intriguing mix of Tilling green and NBC poppy red buses in evidence although all the coaches I saw were in National white livery. The Winchester-based operator R Chisnell & Sons Ltd (trading as King Alfred Motor Services) had been acquired by the National Bus Company, in the guise of Hants & Dorset, during April 1973 and the few vehicles from the Chisnell fleet that had been retained were also being transformed in appearance. Hants & Dorset continued to maintain a depot in

ABOVE LEFT: *Another visit to Bedford Place at Southampton was rewarded by being able to take this photo of 1101 (YRU 75), a Bristol FS6B with ECW body which had been delivered in February 1960. It had been repainted into NBC poppy red livery in August 1973. I felt that the sun visors added character to these buses.* ABOVE RIGHT: *I had a busy itinerary for Wednesday 7 August, so it was an early start from Bournemouth bus station to catch the bus to Southampton. It was still very much a Tilling green scene that morning with just one poppy red bus lurking in the middle of the bus station's parking area. Taking centre stage is 1547 (XEL 833K) a 43-seat ECW bodied Bristol LH6L which was new in 1972. It is looking scruffy with front nearside corner damage which looks as though it also removed the trafficator. It carries its original Tilling-style fleet name rather than the NBC corporate version which had been applied to most vehicles in the Hants & Dorset fleet.*

ABOVE: *Also at Bedford Place was 3093 (163 AUF) an ex-Southdown Weymann-bodied Leyland Leopard PSU3/3RT. New to Southdown in 1963 it was acquired by Hants & Dorset in December 1973. The semi-coach was fresh out of the paint shop after having had the NBC poppy red and white local coach livery applied.*

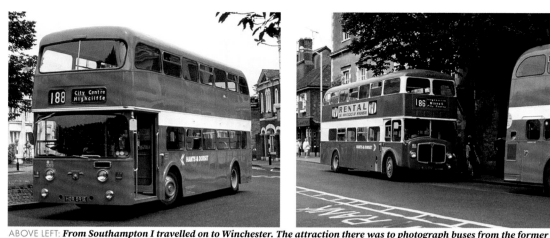

ABOVE LEFT: *From Southampton I travelled on to Winchester. The attraction there was to photograph buses from the former King Alfred fleet. The business was acquired by Hants & Dorset, together with the fleet of 37 vehicles, on April 29, 1973. By the time of my visit seven vehicles had been withdrawn whilst 25 had received NBC bus, dual-purpose, or coach livery. These included 2303 (HOR 591E), a 1967 Roe-bodied Leyland Atlantean PDR1/2. On repaint all four of the batch had their front route number blinds altered to three-track and the side destination indicators were removed.*
ABOVE RIGHT: *I was delighted that I was able to photograph one of the two 1959 Park Royal-bodied Bridgemasters which remained in service, and that this was one of the five buses still in King Alfred livery. 2202 (WCG 107) loads in The Broadway.*

Winchester for routes to Southampton, Andover, Fareham and Salisbury along with the Winchester city services. Hants & Dorset had also taken over the services operated by Western National in Swanage.

There apparently was a shortage of vehicles which had resulted in some unusual acquisitions from Maidstone & District and Southdown and the loan of elderly Bristol LDs from Southern Vectis.

Bournemouth's iconic two-storey bus and coach station was a major attraction for me with the wide variety of vehicles coming and going. Just two years later, on July 25, 1976, a devastating fire would engulf the underground coach station destroying 16 coaches, two cars and a minibus. The intensity of the fire was such that the integrity of the building was compromised making the bus station located above unsafe and the facility was never used again.

During my holiday I took a total of 117 colour slides of buses and coaches; a colourful selection is included here.

ABOVE: *A bus waiting area on Exeter Lane, opposite the coach station exit, was shared by Bournemouth Corporation and Hants & Dorset. Two of the Corporation's November 1964 intake of Leyland Atlantean PDR1/1s with 74-seat Weymann bodies, 170 and 171 (AEL 170/1B), flank one of the pair of unusual MH Cars-bodied Daimler Fleetlines which were new in June 1964. The Fleetlines were 77-seaters.*
LEFT: *I returned to Bournemouth just as various Corporation buses were taking up service for the evening peak. 157 (8157 EL), a 1960 Weymann-bodied Leyland Titan PD3/1 was climbing up Pavilion Road and skirting around the two-storey bus station that was to its left.*

ABOVE: *Approaching Poole bus station, which can just be seen on the left, is Royal Blue 2247 (626 DDV). This 39-seat ECW-bodied Bristol MW6G was new in May 1960 but still looked extremely smart at just over 14 years old. It was part of a batch of 12 coaches.*

LEFT: *On Friday August 9, the final day of my holiday, I had a ride out to Poole. My bus for the journey on service 1 from Bournemouth bus station was 3311 (NRU 311M) a 72-seat ECW- bodied Bristol VRT/SL6G. It was new in February 1974.*

BELOW: *A photo taken of the Hants & Dorset bus station in Bournemouth from an elevated position above Exeter Road reveals a real mix of vehicles in poppy red and Tilling green. Whilst it is not possible to identify specific vehicles the Duple-bodied Bedford VAM14 coach in the foreground is one of the five that were new to Wilts & Dorset in 1967. The new order, in the shape of a poppy red Leyland National, can just be identified by its rear pod towards the back of the parking area.*

In an unusual first for *Buses Yearbook*, regular contributor John Robinson provides a photo-feature in which all the pictures were taken using a smartphone.

Dial-

National Express West Midlands ADL Enviro400 MMCs 6734 (SN15 LEJ) and 6744 (SN15 LHX) in Platinum livery stand in Bull Street, Birmingham on 10 May 2018, my first full day of using the P20 Pro. This view was shot in RAW and subsequently processed in Photoshop; I later discovered that JPEGs taken in the Pro mode produced more than acceptable results with smaller, more manageable, image files.

For those who think from the title that this is going to be an article about those once-fashionable bespoke services that picked up at your front door, often using small van-derived buses, it is not (thankfully, I hear you say!).

Rather, in a first for *Buses Yearbook*, it is a feature where all the photographs have been taken using a smartphone.

As a committed transport photographer for almost fifty years, and one who has always used the manual settings on my cameras to maintain complete control of the picture-taking process, it took a considerable length of time before I considered the mobile phone to be a serious photographic tool.

All that changed in April 2018 when Chinese-manufacturer Huawei released its P20 Pro smartphone, directly aimed at those with a serious interest in photography. Huawei had teamed up

BELOW: *Travel de Courcey operates an extensive network of services in Coventry and beyond. Standing in the bus station at Arena Retail Park on 2 June 2018 are 815 (V325 KGW), a Dennis Trident 2 with Alexander ALX400 bodywork ex Travel London TA25/Abellio London 9725 and 549 (AE54 MWA), a MAN 14.220 with MCV Evolution bodywork purchased new.*

a-bus

At the end of a superb event in Barking on 30 March 2019 commemorating 40 years since London Transport's RTs finished operation, RT3871 (LLU 670), new in 1950, stands at the former 62 terminus at Fullwell Cross, Barkingside, after working the whole of the 1979 62 route from Creekmouth to Barkingside, the final route operated by RTs. Across the road, operating route 169 from Barking to Clayhall, is Stagecoach London ADL Enviro400 19777 (LX11 BFY). Using the P20 Pro's Night mode allowed this dusk image to be taken hand-held, the automatic exposure being 3 seconds at ISO 200 with a fixed aperture of f1.8.

with no less a partner than Leica, the hugely-respected German lens and camera manufacturer, to co-engineer an incredibly capable high-end smartphone with no fewer than three Leica cameras; reviews of the P20 Pro were fantastic which really piqued my interest.

Although I already had a basic smartphone with a camera, I had never taken any photographs with it, using it solely as a phone as I had no real interest in exploring its photographic potential. However, around this time I had purchased a stage-side ticket to see The Rolling Stones play Coventry's Ricoh Arena as part of their European 'No Filter' tour and I needed a decent camera to record the event. The venue had already confirmed to me that large cameras were prohibited, along with bags, so this was the catalyst to purchase my first ever high-end smartphone - the P20 Pro.

The main camera combines a 27mm-equivalent (in 35mm film terms) f1.8 wide-angle lens with a 40 megapixel (MP) 1/1.7" sensor. Additionally, there is a monochrome camera module comprising

a 27mm-equivalent f1.6 wide-angle lens and 20MP 1/2.7" sensor and an 80mm-equivalent f2.4 telephoto lens with an 8MP 1/4" sensor providing 3x optical zoom and 5x hybrid zoom.

Compared to a 35mm 'full-frame' digital sensor, which has an area of 864 square mm (36x24), the main colour sensor of the P20 Pro has an area of just 43.32 square mm (7.6 x 5.7). So, the main sensor covers just five per cent of the area of 35mm 'full-frame'; the sensors in the other two cameras are even smaller yet all can produce outstanding results.

Whilst the monochrome camera can, of course, take dedicated monochrome images it is also designed to operate in conjunction with the other cameras to improve image resolution. Colour images have long been able to be converted to monochrome with in-camera editing or digital software after downloading, but images taken using the dedicated monochrome sensor are vastly superior to converted ones, needing little in the way of processing, and produce beautifully-clean

With the noticeable shutter lag, photographing fast-moving vehicles requires precision timing. Luckily, I managed to frame Stagecoach Volvo B11RT/Plaxton Elite 54304 (YX64 WCG) as intended. It is heading along a comparatively quiet A428 near Cambourne operating the X5 service from Cambridge to Oxford on 17 April 2019.

and detailed results with excellent tonality.

Although all three cameras have fixed apertures there is still plenty of depth of field, equivalent to shooting at 27mm f8 on a full-frame camera.

With these relatively wide-angle lenses, any tilting of the phone up or down when taking a photograph will cause distortion of the subject, manifested as converging or diverging verticals, so it is essential to keep the camera as level as possible, although this is far easier said than done when holding it and framing the picture, especially with a moving subject.

However, moderate amounts of distortion can be corrected by using the Transform Tool in

ABOVE RIGHT: *This Victoria scene, shot through a plate glass window on 17 February 2019, does have a splash of colour courtesy of two impressive Van Hool TX2 Altanos. On the left is Flixbus, Belgium, 293 (1-RBN-638) operating to Brussels whilst alongside is South Gloucestershire Bus & Coach SG35 (KX14 HSO) - also carrying Stagecoach fleet number 55013 - operating Megabus service M6 to Plymouth. Both vehicles are left-hand-drive, the latter vehicle having originally operated with Megabus in Belgium.*

BELOW: *For many years Victoria Coach Station was a rainbow of colours as coaches from myriad operators were to be found there. The scene today, with National Express to the fore, is very uniform such that this line-up of Caetano Levante-bodied coaches on the same day as the previous image, looks much the same whether rendered in colour or, as here, monochrome.*

Photoshop, which allows the image to be digitally tilted up and down thus alleviating any issues. This can only be done with RAW files, although I generally only take JPEGs with the phone (unlike with my DSLRs which are permanently set to record both JPEG and RAW images) but these can subsequently be converted to RAW with the appropriate software once downloaded if this is required.

The camera app has a Pro mode which provides direct control of key exposure settings (ISO, shutter speed and exposure compensation); in this mode the camera can also record DNG (Digital Negative) RAW files although not with the telephoto or monochrome cameras. DNG image files come out at a massive 80MB, compared to around 10-15MB for a colour JPEG taken in Pro mode, so take up much more space in the camera's memory and require a bit of time to digitally process after downloading which I didn't feel justified the effort. Consequently, I find it far easier to shoot JPEGs which, although providing excellent results straight out of the camera, can be given a few tweaks in software (I use Adobe Lightroom and Photoshop together with DxO PhotoLab 2) to give subtle improvements to various parameters such as exposure, contrast and clarity where needed.

The P20 Pro also incorporates several innovative computational photography features such as Artificial Intelligence (AI) which can detect various scenes and tune the camera settings accordingly as well as providing image stabilisation which,

ABOVE: *The monochrome mode really suits older buses. This all-Leyland Titan PD2/3, classified as Leyland 6RT by London Transport, was one of 500 RTWs which entered service in 1949-50. LT's first 8ft-wide motor buses, they were initially allocated to depots operating routes away from Central London due to concerns by the authorities that the extra six inches of width could cause congestion or accidents when they passed on narrow streets or corners. A series of extensive tests in 1950 allayed all such fears and the restriction was lifted. New in 1950, RTW467 (LLU 957) was initially allocated to Battersea garage. The final day of RTW operation was in May 1966 by which time Brixton was the only garage operating the type. RTW467 was the last bus to run in but was happily saved for preservation and 53 years later is seen looking immaculate at the Barking RT event on 30 March 2019. The phone was mounted on an extendible pole to get the high viewpoint.*

BELOW: *Edwards Coaches of Llantwit Fardre has become a major National Express contractor. Waiting in Elizabeth Bridge, London, in February 2019, is this impressive Scania K410UB6/ Caetano Boa Vista, BU18 OTB, one of four new in May 2018.*

The fleet of Souls Coaches, Olney, Buckinghamshire, includes two 3-axle Volvo B9TLs purchased new in 2008 and 2009. The first of these, PO58 KPK, is seen crossing Felmersham Bridge over the River Great Ouse on 21 March 2019 operating a service from nearby Sharnbrook School. Built circa 1818 by public subscription, the bridge was given Grade II listing in May 1952. The high viewpoint was achieved by mounting the 'phone on an extended monopod and firing the shutter with a remote Bluetooth release. Interestingly, although both buses have effectively identical Olympus bodywork, the first is technically an East Lancs product. It was completed before the Darwen Group (which had acquired East Lancashire Coachbuilders in 2007 after they went into administration and subsequently made a reverse takeover of Optare) adopted the Optare name at Blackburn; the second bus carries Optare Olympus bodywork.

amongst other things, enables the provision of a remarkable hand-held night-shot mode. Normally, long hand-held exposures will be rendered unusably-blurred as it is impossible to hold the camera sufficiently steady. Huawei's night-shot mode overcomes this by using AI Image Stabilisation (AIS) which combines both electronic and optical image stabilisation allowing shooting at shutter speeds up to 8 seconds whilst still producing sharp results.

This is achieved by the camera making a series of short exposures which are then aligned and blended together to produce the final image. The image can be seen on the screen as it gradually builds up, with the device balancing light and dark areas of the scene as it goes along. Surely such

innovative technology will find its way into DSLRs and other cameras soon...

The virtual shutter release is on the rear screen of the camera and must be tapped to take the picture. This is counter-intuitive to all other cameras I have used and in the early days of using the camera I did miss a few shots by 'holding' the button down! However, since then I have purchased a hand grip incorporating a removable Bluetooth shutter

RIGHT: *Abellio London New Routemaster LT704 (LTZ 1704) leaves its inner terminus in Cockspur Street, Trafalgar Square, on 17 February 2019 operating route 3 to Crystal Palace. Travelling in the opposite direction is The Original Sightseeing Tour VXE726 (YJ11 TVK), a Volvo B9TL with Optare Olympus open-top bodywork.*

release, which clamps onto the smartphone. This makes holding it far easier than before, as the P20 Pro's slim and smooth profile made gripping it steadily quite challenging. The hand grip also incorporates a tripod thread allowing long exposures to be taken with the phone on a tripod although, to date, I have never used it this way, finding it far easier and less obtrusive to support the phone with a bean-bag for longer exposures which are not taken in the night mode.

There is a very slight delay between tapping the shutter button and the picture being taken (even more so when using the Bluetooth shutter release) so it requires a bit of judgement when taking photographs of moving subjects to ensure the subject is in the required position within the picture. Additionally, in Pro mode, only a single shot can be taken (a burst of shots can be taken with some of the other settings) adding to the on-the-spot planning necessary to ensure the shutter is released at just the right moment to avoid, for example, unwanted vehicles or pedestrians which might be about to enter the frame and ruin the picture. The Bluetooth release, being removable from the grip, allows the shutter to be fired from a distance enabling high-level shots, with the phone

Stagecoach London AEC Routemaster RM2060 (ALM 60B) picks up opposite Cannon Street station on 17 February 2019 operating heritage route 15 from Trafalgar Square to Tower Hill. Two weeks later this service, operated by West Ham garage, was restricted to weekend and bank holiday operation and running only from March to September. Although a night shot this, along with the previous photo, was taken in Pro mode with a manual exposure (1/15 second at ISO250 for this view), which produces a larger image file, the phone being supported against a post with a bean-bag.

BELOW: *An old print re-photographed is this scene taken on 6 March 1980 in Golborne Street, Warrington, now disappeared following extension of the Golden Square shopping centre. Featuring three Warrington Borough Council Daimler Fleetlines, with 30 (HED 857E) nearest the camera and 7ft 6in-wide Leyland Titan PD2/40 50 (BED 731C). All are operating cross-town services which didn't enter the nearby bus station, and all are bodied by East Lancs, Warrington's usual supplier for many years.*

Along with several other NBC subsidiaries, United Counties took lightweight chassis during times of new vehicle shortages in the 1970s, a total of 70 entering the fleet between 1973 and 1976, made up of Bedford YRQ and YRT models and Ford R1014s. Preserved examples of these lightweights are relatively few as they did not have the longevity of the heavyweight buses. However, bucking this trend is 111 (RBD 111M), a YRT with Willowbrook bodywork new in 1974 which made its debut, following an extensive restoration, at the 2019 Wellingborough running day and is seen here on London Road climbing out of Wellingborough at the close of the event on 14 April.

mounted on an extendible pole, to be taken.

Whilst the tiny sensors of a smartphone mean the image quality can never match that of a DSLR, particularly when images are enlarged on the computer screen or in printing, they are still excellent pocket cameras and the P20 Pro produces truly remarkable results, officially recognised by its ranking right at the top of the DxOMark quality ratings along with its sibling, the P20 Pro Mate, which swaps the monochrome camera for a super-wide-angle 16mm-equivalent lens. DxOMark is the leading source of independent image-quality measurements and ratings for smartphones, cameras and lenses since 2008.

As the old saying goes, 'the best camera is the one you have with you', and a smartphone is always likely to be to hand.

RIGHT: *Looking like one of those arty London bus photos, where the bus is rendered red against a monochrome background, this is actually a full-colour view of LT244 (LTZ 1244) in Cheapside in February 2019 where the surroundings just happen to be black and white! The Stagecoach London-operated Wrightbus New Routemaster is on service 8 from Bow to Tottenham Court Road.*